NUTRITION
AND THE
FEEDING OF
HORSES

**This book is to be returned on or before
the last date stamped below.**

1

NUTRITION
AND THE
FEEDING OF
HORSES

Beth Maloney

SWAN·HILL
PRESS

Copyright © 1997 Beth Maloney

First Published in the UK in 1997
by Swan Hill Press, an imprint of Airlife Publishing Ltd

British Library Cataloguing-in-Publication Data
 A catalogue record for this book
 is available from the British Library

ISBN 1 85310 744 1

Typeset by Phoenix Typesetting, Ilkley, West Yorkshire.
Printed in England by Livesey Ltd, Shrewsbury.

Swan Hill Press

an imprint of Airlife Publishing Ltd
101 Longden Road, Shrewsbury SY3 9EB, England

Dedication

This book is dedicated to:
Felix and Oscar who have taught me a vast amount about horses.
My parents for their faith in my abilities.
My sister for her support and friendship.

Acknowledgements

My grateful thanks are due to many people who have encouraged and supported me throughout the research and writing of this book. However, a few that I would specially like to single out are:

Sarah Pilliner for sparking my interest in the subject of nutrition.

Collette Embury for her friendship, support and access to her photograph album.

Wendy Taylor and Giselle Chandler for their kind assistance and photographs.

Michele Thornton for suffering my endless questions, for her support and keeping my spirits up.

Robert Gray for surviving the ordeal!

The equine students and staff at Oakland College for their support and encouragement.

I would like to thank the following people for giving me permission to use or take many photographs of their horses:

Victoria Hughes

Fiona Cotton

Elaine Gray

Debbie Symes

Oaklands College Equestrian Centre

Jessie Graham

Contents

Foreword

The purpose of *Nutrition and the Feeding of Horses* is to provide the horse owner with all the information required to enable them to make knowledgeable decisions about the best diets for their individual horses. It is essential to remember at all times that each horse is an individual, with unique dietary requirements and that this book is simply a guide to assist the owner in understanding the needs of the horse and what is available to fulfil these needs. Up-to-date scientific principles are discussed in layman's terms and put in a form that is easy to understand and use when preparing diets for the horse.

The aim of *Nutrition and the Feeding of Horses* is to simplify the science of feeding and make it an easily obtainable art that any owner or horse person can understand and use in practical day-to-day situations.

The diet of the horse is only one part of the picture when discussing the care and management of horses but knowing how the horse uses feeds, what effect certain feeds have on the horse and general requirement guidelines will greatly assist in keeping your horse healthy, happy and able to perform to the best of their ability.

Introduction

NUTRIENT REQUIREMENTS OF THE HORSE

When attempting to fully understand the nutritional requirements of your horse it is often easier to consider your horse as a machine. In order for this machine to function correctly it needs some kind of fuel, which in this case comes from the food eaten. This food is then converted into energy in the body and the energy is used for very many different functions, rather like petrol in a car. Once all the energy has been removed from the food what is left, the waste, is passed out of the system.

It is also essential that the fuel put into this machine contains all the correct ingredients. If a car has been designed to run on petrol it is not going to get far on diesel! With a horse the food eaten must contain a correct balance of the following nutrients in order for him to 'run' smoothly:

Carbohydrates
Proteins
Fats
Water
Vitamins and minerals.

Finally, it is important that the correct amount of fuel is put in the machine. Too little and the horse will be running low on energy and not performing well, too much and the horse will develop problems with performance and health.

WORK RATES OF HORSES

When assessing the work your horse or pony does it is important to be completely honest! Throughout the book I will be using certain terms and specific definitions which are explained below:

Maintenance   This refers to a horse or pony that is not in work but is not ill or pregnant or lactating. It refers to the energy the horse needs just to stay alive and maintain the health and working order of all the systems.

Light work   This covers daily hacking and schooling for a maximum period of 30 minutes focusing on walk and trot. It includes a horse that is competing occasionally in jumping or dressage at pony or riding club level.

Medium work   This includes regular schooling, regular competing at all disciplines, hunting one day a week and one-day horse trials.

Hard work   This includes competing at two- and three-day events and hunting two days a week.

Fast work   This covers racing.

Dry Matter   Feed that has had all the water removed. This is used when calculating the contents of feeds, such as vitamins and minerals.

Megajoules   This term is a measurement of energy similar to calories.

FORMULATIONS

The following formulations and abbreviations will be used throughout this book.

Abbreviations:

kg	=	kilogram
g	=	gram
mg	=	milligram
MJDE	=	Megajoules of digestible energy

Weights:

1 kg	=	2.205 lb
1 lb	=	0.454 kg
100 g	=	1 kg
1000 kg	=	1 tonne
1 g	=	1000 milligram (mg)
1 mg	=	1000 micrograms (mcg)

International units (this is a unit of measurement used for vitamins):

1 iu of vitamin A	=	0.3 micrograms
1 iu of vitamin D	=	0.025 micrograms
1 iu of vitamin E	=	1 milligram

CHAPTER 1

General Feed Requirements of The Horse

WHY ARE THE NATURAL EATING HABITS OF A HORSE RELEVANT TO FEEDING?

Group of horses

When considering the feed requirements of your horse it is essential that you are aware of how horses ate when they were wild. This is because the horse has evolved over millions of years to survive in a particular environment. This environment consisted of extensive grassland plains containing a wide variety of grasses and other plant species. The horse evolved to exist on a diet of plants but because plant matter is relatively low in nutrients compared to other food stuffs, the horse had to eat vast amounts. Horses are classified as non-ruminant herbivores, meaning they live off plant matter and have a particular digestive system (which we will be discussing in more detail later) that requires plants to be moving through the digestive system continuously. This is why they are called trickle feeders. They regularly need to eat little amounts for approximately 18 hours a day.

Studies have shown that wild horses would eat larger amounts of grass and plant matter during the spring and summer, fattening up on the rich, nutritious spring grass and shoots. They would store this food as layers of fat which would then help them to survive through the winter when grass was less nutritious and in short supply. The wild horses would graze over vast areas of land, eating a variety of grasses, herbs and shrubs providing them with a good variety of nutrients. The herd were always moving onto fresh areas of pasture and were able to select the best grasses and shrubs to fulfil their nutritional needs, and get some exercise on the way!

The wild horse ate enough to provide the amount of energy needed to survive. This is often referred to as a 'maintenance level' as it provides enough energy for the body to function.

All this energy was gained from a 'roughage' diet as the wild horses very rarely came across bowls of oats or coarse mix when wandering across the plains!! As roughage such as grasses and shrubs have a relatively low energy content (you never hear of horses hotting up on hay!) the horse had to eat a large amount to generate the energy levels needed, which was why they would graze for up to 18 hours a day.

The horse's digestive system was designed to make the maximum use of these feed habits and it was very efficient at drawing energy out of stalky, roughage feeds and coping with the horse eating little and often for long periods of time.

Being aware of these points gives the owner an understanding of why it is important to feed horses on a regular basis, feed small amounts throughout the day and try to stay as close to the horse's natural feed habits as possible. They have evolved over millions of years to live this way and are not planning to adapt to domestication for at least another few thousand or more!

CHANGES THAT OCCURRED TO THE DIET WHEN THE HORSE BECAME DOMESTICATED

The domestication of the horse meant that many of these natural feeding habits were lost or altered, mainly due to the fact that the horse's lifestyle and, therefore, feed requirements have changed. For example:

- The horse is required to work much harder and therefore has a greater need for energy from the diet.
- The horse is kept on small paddocks which limit the area available for grazing.
- This limit of space means a more limited selection of grasses and plants.
- Horses are often stabled which means their feed habits are governed entirely by their owner.
- The horse is fed a more consistent diet which does not fluctuate with the seasons.
- Owners prefer their horses to have a trim figure and so limit the amount of roughage in the diet to get rid of the 'grass belly'.

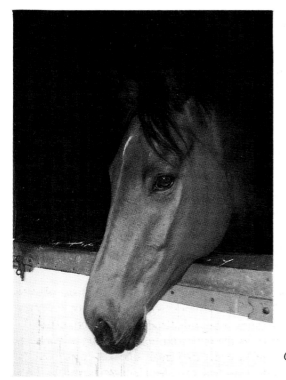

*Changes that occur to diet when
horses became domesticated*

One of the biggest changes that occurred in the diet of the domesticated horse was the increase of concentrate feeds. The horse's increased workload meant an increased energy requirement which could not be supplied through a diet of roughage feeds like grass and hay so a new energy source needed to be added to the horse's diet. This was supplied in the form of concentrate feeds such as oats and barley, mixes and cubes.

Unfortunately the horse's digestive system has not been designed for dealing with buckets of oats or barley and these concentrate feeds can cause health problems such as colic if fed incorrectly.

WHY DO WE FEED CONCENTRATES TO OUR HORSES?

This may seem like a strange question but often owners never consider why they supplement their horse's roughage with concentrate feeds. When asked the answers are often, 'because that's what it was being fed by the old owner', or 'that's what my friends feed their horse', or 'because that's what I have always fed'. We can also be in the habit of putting human values on our horses. Just because we like to eat three large meals a day do our horses really need to?

The answer to such a question should be, 'to provide the nutrients and energy needed to keep the horse healthy and able to perform to the best of his ability'. Every horse should be looked at as an individual and fed according to the work it is doing at the time, not the work it was doing last month or even last year!

In order to be able to supply your horse with all the required nutrients you need to be aware of the factors that can influence the diet of a horse.

FACTORS THAT CAN INFLUENCE YOUR HORSE'S FEED REQUIREMENTS

There are a number of factors that need to be considered when looking at your horse's feed requirements. These factors will influence how much feed your horse will need and what type of feed will be suitable.

Health
If your horse is in good health the demands put upon all the body systems will be minimal and your feed will be used to maintain a healthy body. If the horse is ill, extra demand will be put on the feed as the body will have an increased demand for certain nutrients.

If the horse is suffering from a virus such as a cold or influenza many cells will be damaged and the horse will probably lose weight. There will be an increased demand for protein to help renew and repair the body and an extra demand for vitamins and minerals. The horse will also require energy for all the repair work that needs to be done.

Ill horses are often off their food so they need a carefully selected diet which supplies all the correct nutrients but is also tempting and easy to eat. This will be looked at in more detail in Chapter 7.

Condition
The weight of your horse is closely linked with the diet. In simple terms your horse will become fatter if you overfeed, and your horse will become thinner if you under feed. Unfortunately it is not as simple as this because it is not just the amount you may be feeding but the choice of feeds. For example, feeding a large quantity of a poor quality feed or low energy feed may not fulfil the horse's energy requirements and he will lose weight. On the other hand if you feed small quantities of a very rich, high energy feed the amount fed is small but the horse may still become fat as the energy content is above the horse's requirements.

When assessing your horse's condition it is very important that you are objective. Many owners tend to be on the generous side when estimating their horse's

'Condition'

condition as they enjoy seeing their horse looking 'well' but it is a fine line between looking well and getting fat!

The easiest way to assess your horse's condition in an objective manner is to use condition scoring and ideally to get someone else to score your horse! This method was originally designed for farm animals and has been altered for the horse. It requires you to score three areas of the body, noting the amount of flesh on each area and then decide upon an overall condition score. It is important that you do not compare the horse you are scoring with other horses when deciding upon a figure. You must treat every horse as an individual. Each area of the body should be given an individual score, the three scores are then added together and divided by three to get the average. This average score is your horse's overall condition score. (Refer to Table 1.1)

Age

The age of a horse does have some bearing on the amount and type of food required. A young horse who is growing and developing has a high requirement for protein and energy and must have a balance of vitamins and minerals. The young horse will therefore have a higher requirement than a mature horse.

The older horse also has particular requirements. Some older horses may start to lose weight, especially in the winter so may require a higher level of energy. The older horse can have teeth problems and only be able to eat certain feeds that do not require heavy chewing!

Work done

In simple terms the more work a horse does the more energy he will require. A working horse needs to convert the energy supplied in his feed into fuel for the body. Different disciplines require different levels of work and muscle power and the diet must reflect this.

Table 1.1 Condition scoring for horses

Score	Spine	Pelvis	Shoulder and Neck
1 Poor	Vertebrae projecting and sharp to touch. Ribs very prominent.	Very angular and sharp hip bones. Deep cavities around tail.	Very thin, ewe necked appearance. No fat between skin and bone.
2 Very thin	Backbone easily seen. Skin tight over bones. All ribs visible.	Pelvis prominent but some cover. Depressions under tail.	Very narrow especially at base. Bones of wither and shoulder clearly visible.
3 Thin	Some fat build up over spine and ribs. Bones can be felt on pressure but not seen.	Hip bones defined but not prominent. Bones easily felt. Slightly angular appearance.	Narrow but firm. Shoulderblade prominent.
4 Moderately thin	Spine covered, no bony areas, ribs are covered but can be felt very easily.	Less angular in appearance. Croup defined. Bones all covered in flesh but can be felt on pressure.	Shoulder and neck blend into body. Light covering of flesh.
5 Moderate	Spine and ribs well covered but can be felt easily on pressure.	Whole area rounded and covered evenly in flesh.	Correct width for body and in proportion.
6 Fleshy	Crease down spine, fat can be seen between ribs.	Very rounded appearance and bones only felt on firm pressure. Gutter seen over croup.	Slight crest on neck, neck firm and wide, possible folds of fatty tissue.
7 Fat	Prominent layer of fat along spine. Ribs have thick covering of flesh.	Pelvis buried in fat and fat deposited on inner buttocks.	Very thick neck with fat deposits over shoulders.
8 Over Fat	Obvious gutter down spine. Ribs hidden by layers of fat.	Pelvis buried in firm fatty tissue and bones can not be felt. Deep gutter along croup.	Bulging fat along withers, behind shoulder and along neck. Thick crest possible.

Adapted from Henneke et al (1983) Equine vet. J. 15

'Work done'

The energy requirement of the working horse can be affected not only by the work done but also by other factors such as:

- The speed of the work – the faster the work the more energy will be used.
- The duration of the work – the longer the time the more energy used.
- The going – soft going is harder work than firm.
- The weather – working in cold weather with the horse working into a wind will require more energy than warm, still days.
- The incline – hills are harder work than flat land.
- The weight of the rider – a heavy rider will use more of the horse's energy.
- Rider ability – advanced riders will work horses harder than a novice rider.

Temperament

A horse's temperament and behaviour can have a direct effect on their diet.

A highly-strung, easily stressed horse will burn up more energy than a lethargic, laid-back horse. Like people, if someone is always stressed and excitable they use up more energy even when they are not doing anything. A horse with a highly-strung temperament is usually difficult to keep weight on as they are using a higher amount of energy, but if given too much energy in the feed they become even more highly-strung.

A laid-back horse who tends to be lazy may need a higher energy feed to pep him up, but again if given too much energy he will put on weight and probably become even more sluggish.

17

Breed

Certain breeds of horse seem to use their feed better than others. Of course this is a generalisation and there are always horses that do not follow the rules but, generally speaking, the native breeds do better on small amounts of feed than the Thoroughbred types. Native ponies and horses, cob types and many Warmbloods are usually prone to putting on too much weight and seem to do very well on hay and small levels of concentrate feed, even when in medium work. The Thoroughbred and Arab type horses tend to need higher levels of energy and can be prone to losing weight very easily, especially when in hard work and during spells of cold weather.

Size

This is self-explanatory: the larger the animal the more feed it will require. This is not just in height but also body type and weight. The weight of a horse gives a useful guideline to the amount of food that horse will require. The general guideline is that a horse's appetite should be 2.5 per cent of the body weight. This provides a maximum figure, as appetite means you totally fulfil your desire for food – if you ate all you could every day you would probably start to go off your food after a few weeks! It is usual to feed horses to just below appetite so that they are always interested in their next meal.

'The seasons'

Your eye

This is probably the most important factor of all! It is essential that you keep a close eye on your horse's general condition on a regular basis and make adjustments to the diet accordingly.

The seasons

A horse will have a higher requirement for energy and, therefore, food during cold, wet and windy conditions, especially if the horse is living out.

A clipped horse in the winter will also have an increased energy requirement in order to maintain body temperature. During the winter and autumn there is less food value in the grass and horses living out will need some extra feed in the form of hay and/or concentrates.

When the weather is very warm and humid horses in work will sweat more and this can increase their need for water and certain minerals. During the spring and summer the grass has a high nutrient level and this will have a direct effect on the diet of horses living out.

The environment

The place where you keep your horse will have an effect on his dietary requirements.

A horse that is fully stabled cannot help himself to feed and is entirely dependent on you. He relies on the owner to provide all the required nutrients in his feeds and if the owner does not supply these the horse will develop deficiencies.

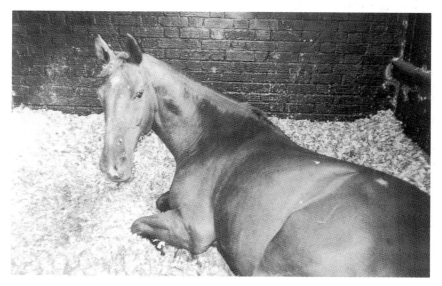

'The stabled horse'

19

The grass-kept horse has different nutritional demands to the stabled horse. In the spring and summer the owner needs to keep a close eye on the grass quality. A flush of spring grass can bring on bouts of colic and laminitis and a dry spell can lead to parched land and a lack of grass. In the winter you need to ensure the horse or pony is getting enough nutrients as the grass loses much of its feed value. A horse wintering out will require hay and possibly concentrates depending on the weather conditions, condition of the horse, work done and quality of the hay fed.

ENERGY REQUIREMENTS OF THE HORSE

What is energy?

Energy is a difficult aspect of a diet to fully understand as it cannot be seen. It is present in all feeds and the results of feeding high levels of energy can be all too apparent when horses become full of themselves. But what is it?

Energy is the life of all cells in the body. It enables things to happen such as breathing, moving and even eating, so it is therefore an essential part of the horse's diet. It is obtained from a variety of sources such as light, heat, chemicals in the cells and electrical impulses in the body. The horse, like other living organisms, can convert one form of energy into another and use it to perform functions that are necessary for survival.

Sources of energy

The horse's main source of energy is from the carbohydrate content of plants. Plants gain their energy from sunlight and convert it into chemical energy to use for growth and maintenance. When the horse eats the plants this chemical energy is passed to the horse. The horse then transfers this energy into many different forms for use throughout the body. It can even be stored in cells and kept until required in the form of adenosine triphosphate (ATP).

Energy demand

All horses needs a certain amount of energy to stay alive and this is often referred to as maintenance energy requirements. Energy demand is also affected by a number of other factors including:

- Temperament – a highly-strung horse can have twice the energy requirement as a calm horse doing the same work.
- Temperature and humidity – cold weather increases energy demand as does high humidity or very hot weather.
- The work required of the horse – the harder the work the more energy is needed.
- The weight of the rider – a heavier rider will make the horse work harder, so increase energy requirements.

Energy: uses in the body

The energy gained from food is lost in many ways and very little of the original gross energy is used for work, as seen in Figure 1.1 below.

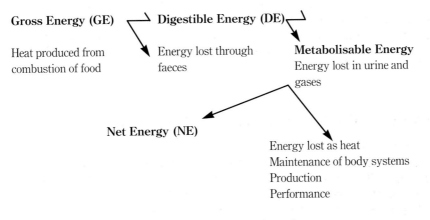

Figure 1.1 How energy is used

How energy is measured

Energy fed to horses is calculated in megajoules of digestible energy (MJDE), a measurement similar to calories. When designing diets for horses you are basically calorie counting. All feeds contain energy and when calculating a balanced diet for your horse you must be aware of the energy needs of your horse and which feeds will supply the correct amount of megajoules to fulfil the requirement. This process will be discussed in detail in Chapter 3.

The ways energy can be used by a horse

All food eaten by the horse, both roughage and concentrates, contains a certain amount of energy. This energy is released when the food is digested in the digestive system. The energy is then available for use in the body. It is similar to filling your car up with petrol, the car will not perform on an empty tank!

This energy can be used for:

- Maintaining all the internal systems and keeping them functioning. For example, circulatory system, respiratory system and even the digestive system.
- Repairing the body when injured or damaged.
- Renewing body cells and tissues.
- Getting rid of waste products from the body.
- Keeping the horse warm.
- Physical work.
- Growth and development of youngsters.
- Providing milk to suckling foals.

Therefore a 15 hh, three-year-old horse living out in the winter and being worked every day will have a greater energy requirement than a 15 hh, ten-year-old horse being rested in the summer.

Research has shown that the energy requirement of horses who are not in work (maintenance energy levels) is proportional to their bodyweight. Therefore a 500 kg horse will need approximately double the energy of a 250 kg pony, although ponies tend to be more efficient at utilising the feeds so often get more nutrients out of the same amount of feed as a horse. Of course this alters dramatically when the horse is working or has other energy demands such as growing or recovering from illness.

Table 1.2 Energy demands for the horse and pony

MJDE a Day

Work done	200 kg pony	600 kg horse
Maintenance requirements	35	78
1 hour walk work	0.4	1.3
1 hour trot at 200 mpm and brief canter work	4.2	12.5
1 hour trot at 220 mpm, canter at 400 mpm and jumping	10.5	31
Riding club one-day event	25	75
Fast work	42	127

Adapted from Horse Nutrition and Feeding *by Sarah Pilliner (1993)*

Feeding excess energy

This situation can occur in two ways:

1. Your horse or pony has a sudden large intake of feed, for example, he breaks into the feedroom and helps himself to the coarse mix! This sudden large intake of concentrate feed will overfill the stomach. The feed will therefore be pushed out into the intestines only partially digested and may result in digestive upsets such as diarrhoea, colic or laminitis.

2. Your horse or pony is given small excesses of feed over a period of weeks or months. If a horse is continually overfed most of the surplus will be stored in the body as fat. Horses have a unique way to get rid of excess energy through exercise. They are the only animal to increase levels of exercise to compensate for increased energy intake. If this exercise is not provided by the owner the horse will make its own, which usually involves leaping and bucking through the air! In addition to increased amounts of body fat and high spirits, youngstock will increase their rate of growth. This spurt of growth can be a cause of Developmental Orthopaedic Disease (DOD).

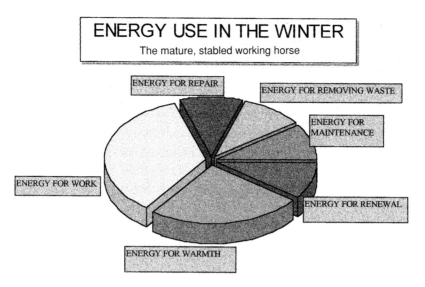

Figure 1.2 Use of energy in the horse in spring and winter

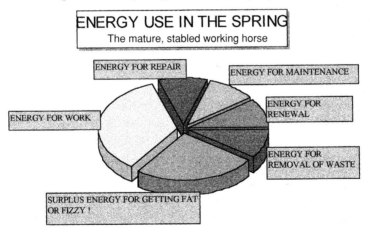

Being overweight causes health problems to the horse, these include:

- Decreased physical performance.
- Increased sweating when exercising. The excess body fat insulates the horse so there is a decreased ability to cool down.
- Strain on respiratory system as the excess body mass increases oxygen needs but decreases the horse's ability to take in oxygen.
- Joint and locomotion problems.

23

Feeding too little energy

There are a number of situations that may cause a horse to have an energy deficiency, these include:

- Insufficient amounts of food offered to the horse.
- The food being offered is too low in energy so the horse cannot eat enough to provide the level of energy required.
- The horse is not eating due to teeth problems or a mouth injury.
- The horse is off his food, possibly due to stress, illness or poor quality food.

Inadequate energy provision causes a hormonal change in the body of the horse. This triggers the body to conserve the energy that is still available so there is a reduction in physical activity, milk production and growth rate. The body is also encouraged to use the stores of body fat for energy, which results in a loss of bodyweight and condition.

If the horse continues to be deficient in energy after using up all the stored fat, he will turn to the body's only remaining energy store, protein. The protein in the blood, muscles, intestines, ligaments and tendons start to be used, which has serious implications on the organs that are losing their protein. The physical signs of this severe lack of energy are:

- Bone and muscle weakness
- Muscle wastage
- Impaired nutrient digestion and absorption
- Impaired immune system so horse is more likely to pick up diseases
- Impaired respiration and circulation.

If a horse has reached this level of malnutrition you need to be very careful when attempting to replenish the energy deficiency. The feed needs to be built up very gradually so as not to overstrain any of the weakened systems.

CHAPTER 2
The Essential Nutrients

AN INTRODUCTION TO NUTRIENTS

The whole of the horse's body from the hair down to the hooves is made from cells. These cells need chemical substances to keep them healthy and functioning correctly. These chemical substances are supplied by the food eaten and are classed as nutrients.

What are nutrients
Both plants and animals are made up of similar chemical substances which can be grouped into components called nutrients which are classified according to their structure and function. These components come from the food eaten.

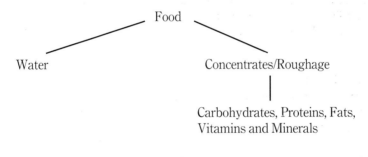

Figure 2.1 The components of food

How do plants provide nutrients to the horse
The horse is a herbivore and therefore gains nutrients from plants or plant products. In order to understand how the horse receives these nutrients from the plants it is necessary to look at how the plant receives its own nutrients.

Grass is probably the most common plant source, so this will be used as the example. The grass grows in the soil in the field. This soil contains a variety of nutrients such as potassium, nitrogen, lime, phosphorous and water. These nutrients are absorbed by the roots of the grass and are taken up into the leaves. Here they are combined with sunlight and carbon dioxide taken from the air and converted into energy. This process is known as photosynthesis. The grass then stores this energy for use when it is growing. The horse then eats this grass and makes use of the energy the plant has made and all the nutrients absorbed by the plant from the soil are passed on to the horse for use in the body.

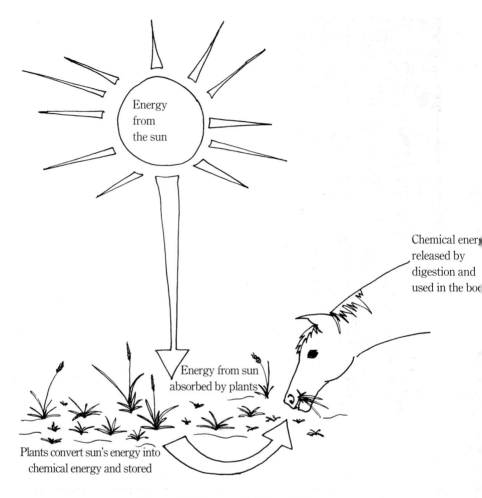

Figure 2.2 Diagram of photosynthesis

CARBOHYDRATES

Carbohydrates are fed to the horse in a large variety of feeds. The majority of the horse's diet is in the form of carbohydrates and this makes them the main source of energy.

Use in the body

The horse uses carbohydrates for one important function, the supply of energy. Carbohydrates provide 80–90 per cent of the energy required by the horse.

Horse in work

Structure

Carbohydrates are a mixture of the chemical elements carbon, hydrogen and oxygen. The hydrogen and oxygen are in the same proportion as for water, hence the name 'hydrates'. These chemicals join up in a number of different combinations to provide a large variety of carbohydrates but they tend to be classified in two main groups:

Simple (soluble) carbohydrates (also called sugars)

- **MONOSACCHARIDES**: simple sugars. These are the most basic sugars and all simple carbohydrates break down into monosaccharides when digested in the body. Examples are:

  FRUCTOSE found in plants.

  GLUCOSE found in cereals and grains.

  GALACTOSE found in milks.

  These sugars provide a fast source of energy when fed as they need very little digestion and are quickly absorbed into the bloodstream due to their basic structure.

27

- **DISACCHARIDES**: these are called double sugars as they are made of two mono-saccharides. Examples are:
  SUCROSE this is the sugar processed from sugar cane or sugarbeet.
  LACTOSE found in the milk of mammals (mare's milk).
  MALTOSE found in cereals.
  These disaccharides are broken down into monosaccharides during digestion.

Complex carbohydrates (also known as starches or roughage)

- **POLYSACCHARIDES**: these are formed from a varying number of monosaccharides. Three main forms are found in the horse's diet:
  STARCH found in plants and cereals.
  CELLULOSE the fibre content of all plants. This gives the plant structure.
  LIGNIN this is the indigestible fibre found in plants.
  GLYCOGEN this is formed from glucose and stored in the liver and muscles after digestion has occurred.

The horse obtains its supply of both types of carbohydrates from the plants eaten. The majority of traditional horse feeds are very high in carbohydrates.

Sources of carbohydrate
Simple carbohydrate feeds. These are found in cereal feeds (the concentrates of the diet). For example, oats, barley, maize, peas and beans, concentrate mixes and cubes. These simple carbohydrate feeds are digested in the small intestine and provide energy in the form of sugars such as glucose, which generate an instant source of energy.
Complex carbohydrate feeds. These are found in the roughage part of the diet. For example, hay, alfalfa, cellulose in plants and grasses. These complex carbohydrates are digested in the hind gut and provide a source of energy in the form of volatile fatty acids, which provide a slow release source of energy.

General requirements
The requirements of carbohydrate feeds in the horse's diet is directly linked to the energy requirements of the individual horse which needs to be calculated from the bodyweight of the horse. These calculations are dealt with in Chapter 7.

Problems
The overfeeding of simple carbohydrates is the most common problem and can lead to:

- Overloading the small intestine resulting in poor digestion of feeds and eventually colic.
- The horse becoming overweight.
- Laminitis.

- Feeding poor quality roughages can also lead to colic and other digestive disturbances.

PROTEIN

This nutrient is an essential part of all living cells and is the most important component of all animal tissues.

Use in the body
Protein is used in the body for:

- Growth of new cells and tissues.
- Growth of youngstock and the production of muscle tissue.
- Repair and renewal of all cells in the body.
- Can be used for energy when fed in excess but not very efficient in this role.

Protein is especially important therefore in the diets of pregnant mares and growing youngstock who have a higher requirement.

A foal has very special protein requirements

Structure
Protein is an organic substance and comes in very many forms. Muscle, tendons, skin, hair and hooves are all made of protein as are many other structures in the body. Each protein is formed from mixtures of the following chemicals:

- Nitrogen (N)
- Hydrogen (H)
- Oxygen (O)
- Phosphorous (P)
- Sulphur (S).

Every protein contains approximately 16 per cent nitrogen and it is the nitrogen content that is used when foodstuffs are analysed for protein content. Each animal has its own specific proteins and there are a very wide variety found in the horse.

Proteins are classified in three groups:

Globular proteins. These are the enzymes, hormones and, antigens (that form antibodies) found in the body.

Fibrous proteins. These are animal proteins. This group contains:

  Collagens makes up about 30 per cent of the protein in the horse's body and is found in many tissues.

  Elastin found in the elastic tissues such as tendons, arteries and muscles.

  Keratin found in hooves and hair. Usually rich in sulphur.

Complex proteins. Also known as compound proteins. These proteins contain some other substance which is attached to the amino acid chain. The extra substance varies, some examples being: a carbohydrate, a lipid or a pigment. Examples of complex proteins are:

  Haemoglobin found in the blood (protein + pigment).

  Mucus used as lubricants in the body (protein + carbohydrates).

AMINO ACIDS

Every protein is made up from simple units called amino acids. These are the building blocks of protein and approximately twenty are recognised as the 'individual' blocks. A selection of the twenty amino acids join together in a chain formation, rather like a necklace. Each necklace will be made of different combinations of these twenty necklace 'beads' (amino acids) and every complete necklace is a form of protein, so there are countless combinations.

The twenty amino acids are classified in two groups:

1. Non-essential amino acids. These amino acids are needed by the horse but are easily available in the diet as they can be made up in the body of the horse. To do this the horse initially eats the proteins from plant sources. These plant proteins are then digested, broken down during digestion into the individual amino acids and then altered in the body. The horse changes them from plant amino acids into 'horse' amino acids for use by the cells.

2. Essential amino acids. These, as their name suggests, are essential to the horse because it cannot make them from other sources. The food fed to the horse must contain them if they are to be provided in the diet. There are ten amino acids that are classed as essential.

1)   An amino acid chain broken down by digestion of **protein** from the feed.

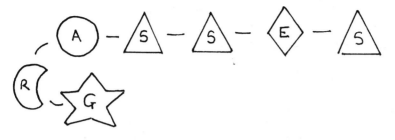

2)   This amino acid chain is broken down into components by enzyme digestion.

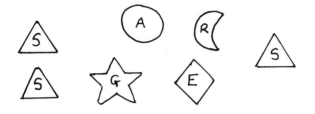

3)   These amino acids are absorbed into the bloodstream and passed into the body. Here they are joined up in a form the horse can use in the body, and fulfil protein requirements.

4)   The amino acid chain was lacking in certain amino acids that the horse needed to complete his requirements.
   So the horse needs to be fed an 'essential amino acid'.

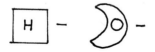

6)   This essential amino acid when digested completes the horse's requirements.

Figure 2.3 The digestion of amino acid chains in simplified diagrammatic form

31

It is the essential amino acids that cause most concern to the horse owner as they *must* be supplied in the feed so that the horse does not become deficient and suffer poor health.

The essential amino acids are:

LYSINE
The 'limiting' amino acid. This essential amino acid is the most important as without lysine the other amino acids cannot be used correctly and so it affects all the protein available to the horse. Lysine is necessary for milk production, correct growth in youngstock, and the formation of the proteins collagen (in tissues), fibrin (for blood clotting), and keratin (for strong hooves).

METHIONINE
Necessary for the formation of the protein keratin (healthy hooves).

ARGENINE
Necessary to maintain correct blood constituency and healthy circulatory system. Also associated with the nucleic acid found in all cells.

HISTIDINE
Necessary for maintaining correct blood constituency and is connected with correct growth pattern in young horses. Also forms histamine which is associated with allergic reactions and infections.

PHENYLALANINE
This is converted into the non-essential amino acid tyrosine and it is necessary for the formation of the hormones adrenaline and thyroxine.

TRYPTOPHAN, LEUCINE, ISOLEUCINE, VALINE AND THREONINE
Are all necessary for growth in youngstock and maintaining a balance of nutrients in the body and the general health of all cells in the body.

Table 2.1 Lysine content of feedstuffs

Feed	Lysine content in %
Brewer's yeast	3.23
Soyabean meal	2.9
Dried skimmed milk powder	2.54
Linseed	1.16
Alfalfa hay	0.79–0.81
Alfalfa meal	0.63–0.85
Sugarbeet	0.54
Barley	0.40
Oats	0.33–0.44
Maize	0.25

Adapted from Nutritional Requirements of Horses.

If a horse's diet is deficient in some or all of the essential amino acids it will not only cause a deficiency which will affect the overall health of the horse but it will also stop the non-essential amino acids from working correctly.

Sources

Feed sources that contain a high level of essential amino acids are classified as feeds with a high biological value. Examples of feeds that are of a high biological value are: Alfalfa (Lucerne), good quality grasses such as Timothy and rye, soyabean meal, linseed, field beans (*Vicia faba*), field peas (*Pisum aruense*), milk, bone meal and fish meal.

Table 2.2 Examples of the protein content in horse feeds

Feed	Crude protein %
Soyabean meal	44
Brewer's yeast	43
Linseed	34.6
Alfalfa meal	16–17
Barley	10–11
Oats	9–12
Maize	9
Sugarbeet	9
Italian rye grass: hay	8
Timothy grass: hay	6–8
Italian rye grass pasture	4
Timothy grass: pasture	3

Adapted from Nutritional Requirements of Horses.

Any cooking process, especially at high temperatures, can reduce the amount of amino acids in the feed source.

Feeding protein

Protein is an essential component of any horse's diet but certain horses have an increased demand or need for protein. Any horse that is growing or developing will need a good level of protein as will pregnant and lactating mares. Horses recovering from injury or illness will require protein in order to repair and renew the damaged tissues and cells.

Research has been carried out on feeding specific amino acids to competition horses. The results have shown that feeding the amino acids carnitine, glutamine, valine, leucine and isoleucine to working horses can reduce the heart rate and the build-up of lactic acid in the muscles, thus delaying fatigue and increasing stamina and endurance. Faster and more effective recovery of the body after strenuous exercise has also been demonstrated.

The protein requirements of a horse are referred to as a percentage of the diet.

33

It is also generally described as crude protein, which can be rather misleading. Crude protein is the total amount of protein that is found in the food but not all this protein is actually used by the horse. Some of this crude protein will never get to the tissues as not all of it is digestible. The ideal would be to know how much digestible protein is in the food but this is very rarely calculated. This means that the requirements for the horse are discussed as crude protein levels as a percentage of the diet.

In most feeds the crude protein level is stated on the label attached to the sack. The amounts of protein in the common feedstuffs will be discussed in a later chapter.

Table 2.3 Crude protein level in percentage of diet

Horse	Crude protein level %
Maintenance (refer to introduction)	7.0–8.0
Light work	7.5–8.0
Medium work	8.0–9.0
Hard work	9.0–10.0
Fast work	9.5–10.0
Pregnancy: 9th month	8.9
Pregnancy: 10th month	9.0
Pregnancy: 11th month	9.5
Foal: first 3 months of lactation	12
Foal: next 3 months of lactation	10
Weanling	13
Yearling: 12–18 months	11
Yearling: 18–24 months	10
Yearling: 24–48 months	10

Adapted from Nutritional Requirements of Horses.

Problems
If protein is overfed it will be broken down (deaminated) in the liver and excreted as urea in the urine. Continued overfeeding of protein can lead to problems such as filled legs, lumps on the skin and liver disorders. Early signs that a horse is being fed too much protein can be an increase in urination and a higher water intake. There can also be a strong smell of ammonia in the urine of stabled horses.

FAT AND OILS (LIPIDS)

All horse feeds contain a certain amount of fat but this has traditionally been a small amount of no more than 6 per cent. Fat is an excellent source of energy in the diet and generates more than twice that of an equal weight of carbohydrates.

Use in the body

Fats and oil are used in the body for:

- Work and reserves of energy
- Insulation and warmth
- Increasing or maintaining condition and weight
- A source of fat soluble vitamins A, D, E and K
- A source of essential fatty acids.

The horse's diet usually has a low fat content and because of this fat has generally been a minor source of energy compared to carbohydrates.

Structure

Fats are composed of the chemical elements carbon (C), hydrogen (H) and oxygen (O). These elements are combined to form two substances: fatty acids and glycerol. There are at least forty fatty acids recognised but it is not yet known which of the fatty acids are essential in the diet.

Fatty acids are further classified as unsaturated and saturated. We tend to feed unsaturated fats to horses as they are from plant sources and are more easily digested. Unsaturated fats are in the form of liquids at room temperature and so are fed as oils. One problem with unsaturated fats is that they can easily turn rancid. To make the oil last longer many feed manufacturers add a synthetic form of vitamin E into the oil which acts as an antioxidant and reduces the chance of the oil becoming rancid.

Three of the more common unsaturated fatty acids are linoleic, linolenic and arachidonic acids. Like the essential amino acids these three fatty acids need to be included in the feed as the horse cannot form them in the body.

Horses have been found to be very effective at digesting and using fat in the body, but the body does need to be 'trained' to store and use fats effectively as a source of energy instead of relying on the carbohydrate sugars. It is only recently that research into fats has taken place and it is now being thought that fats can provide a useful solution to supplying high levels of energy to competition horses without the drawbacks of high carbohydrate diets. Fats are now being used at up to 6–7 per cent in the diets of high performance and endurance horses.

Feeding fats

There are no recommended general requirements for fats and oils. Most traditional horse diets contain 2–3 per cent fat. Most owners find that adding up to 90 ml (3 oz) of vegetable oil will provide all the necessary fatty acids and can improve the condition of the coat and skin. An 8 oz measure of oil added to the diet of a competition horse will provide the same amount of digestible energy as 700 g (1.5 lb) of oats. Feeding fats to competition horses has been shown to improve stamina and endurance and feeding fats to lactating broodmares increases the fat content in their milk, so improving the condition of their foals.

Sources

Table 2.4 Feeds rich in fats and oils

Feed	Content of fat in %
Vegetable oil	98.0
Linseed oil	36.0
Oats	5.1
Maize	3.6
Alfalfa hay	2.6
Timothy hay	2.5

Problems

Feeding more than 12 per cent fat in the diet can lead to intestinal disorders, diarrhoea and increased levels of cholesterol in the blood. Overfeeding fats and oils can also cause problems such as excess energy or an increase in weight as excess fat is stored in the body, which can lead to extra strain on the heart, lungs and limbs.

VITAMINS

Vitamins are essential in any diet but are usually not given much thought as they are required in very small quantities and are often contained in the feeds given to horses.

Use in the body

Vitamins are necessary for the body to function and perform at all levels from maintaining a glossy coat to keeping the nervous system functioning correctly. The specific uses of each vitamin are stated further on.

Structure

There are sixteen vitamins that are used by the body for numerous functions which are discussed in this chapter.

Vitamins are classified as:

FAT-SOLUBLE: A, D, E and K. These vitamins are dissolved in fat and can be stored in the liver or fat cells for use later. This means that these vitamins can be fed in excess and an overdose can easily occur.

WATER-SOLUBLE: B-complex and C. These vitamins are dissolved in water and are stored in the body for a very short time. Excess amount of water soluble vitamins are excreted if overfed so overdosing is uncommon. Because only a limited amount are stored these vitamins must be provided on a daily basis in the diet. Most water soluble vitamins are supplied in the feed or made in the intestines of the horse.

Feeding vitamins

All the vitamins need to be provided in the diet but some are made by the bacteria in the horse's intestine or in the liver and so do not need to be fed. The requirements of vitamins are related to growth rate, age, reproductive status and the work done by the horse.

Overdosing particular vitamins can be as problematic as having a deficiency. An overdose can occur when feeding specific vitamins if you do not know what is being provided in the feed and which vitamin is deficient. An overdose can even cause deficiencies in other nutrients as it unbalances the whole diet and can lead to toxicity.

If a horse is being fed good quality feeds which are designed to meet all the specific requirements it is very unlikely to require any vitamin supplementation as it should be receiving all the required vitamins in the diet.

Vitamin A: retinol

Functions

- Maintains moisture in the mucous membranes of all systems and health of epithelial tissues.
- Used to form visual purple which is used in retina of the eye for vision in dull light.
- Required for healthy bone growth, tissue development and blood cell formation.

Feeding requirements

It is very rare for horses to become deficient in vitamin A as there is a high level of carotene in pasture land which is the main source in a grazing horse's diet. It is also stored in the liver and fat tissues of the body. The only horses at risk of deficiency tend to be horses that are stabled and never given any fresh green feeds, cod liver oil or a mix or cubes which contain vitamins and minerals.

Because vitamin A is stored and easily available in pasture land there is a risk of overfeeding. Excess feeding (over 16,000 iu per kg of feed) can lead to:

- Increased weakness in bones
- Loss of hair and poor skin
- Changes in red blood cell concentrations
- Inco-ordination.

Vitamin D: calciferol

Functions

- Aids in the absorption, uptake and transport of calcium and phosphorous.

- Vitamin D is relatively inactive until it is stimulated by parathormone. This is secreted from the parathyroid gland in the neck. Parathormone converts the vitamin D into an active form in the kidney. It is now in the form of a steroid hormone.

   It has two target areas: small intestine and bone. When in the kidney it stimulates the reabsorption of calcium ions and blocks the reabsorption of phosphates. In the small intestine it stimulates the absorption of calcium and phosphorous in the food. In the bone it mobilises the bone minerals to enable them to move to other parts of the body if necessary, or to add calcium and phosphate ions.

Vitamin D provitamins

A provitamin is a substance that does not have a vitamin value. It must be converted into a vitamin in the body in order to have any value. There are two vitamin D provitamins: ergosterol and 7-dehydro-cholesterol. These substances are converted into vitamin D when exposed to ultra-violet light. This can be achieved through the skin.

Feed requirements

Because vitamin D is generated by sunlight, any grazing horses are very unlikely to need supplementation. Young, growing horses may require some supplementing if they are not getting grass or coarse mixes which contain added vitamins and minerals. Rugged and stabled horses, especially in indoor stables, will have the greatest requirement and again you need to check what feeds you are providing to ensure they receive enough vitamin D in the diet.

   As with vitamin A, excess vitamin D is stored in the liver and fat tissues so overfeeding is a possible problem. If you feed over 2,500 iu/kg of dry matter it can result in:

- Swelling of joints.
- Weakened bones and increased occurrence of fractures.
- Soft tissues in the body turning into bone (calcification).
- The skull and jaw can become enlarged.
- In severe cases can poison the horse.

Vitamin E: tocopherol

Functions
- Acts as an antioxidant protecting the body cells from toxic 'oxides' and protects unsaturated lipids in the tissue from oxidation.
- This antioxidant quality is very important in competition horses as the vitamin prevents the formation of toxic substances in working horses when the muscles are working hard.
- Works with selenium as a body tissue 'stabiliser' ensuring the stability of red blood cells.
- Recently thought to play a role in the development and function of the immune system.

Feed requirements
Vitamin E is stored in the body but does not store as well as vitamins A and D. Horses that have higher requirements of vitamin E tend to be competition horses that are under stress, and stud stock as it is connected with fertility.

If a horse is being fed a high level of oil or fat in the diet, an increased requirement of vitamin E will be needed: 5 mg/kg vitamin E of every 1 per cent fat above 3 per cent of ration.

To date there have been no documented problems related to the overfeeding of vitamin E.

Vitamin K

Functions
- Required for effective blood clotting.
- Vitamin K is necessary for the synthesis of prothrombin in the liver. Prothrombin is a preliminary form of thrombin, an enzyme. This enzyme converts the protein fibrinogen in blood plasma into fibrin that is used in blood clotting and scab formation.

Feed requirements
Horses rarely require vitamin K as it is synthesised by the gut flora. This supply is usually sufficient. Extra amounts may be needed when a horse is on a blood anti-coagulant, for example, Dicumerol, or has been ill and suffering diarrhoea. Some people consider that a horse diagnosed as a bleeder may be helped by supplementation with vitamin K.

Table 2.5 Fat-soluble vitamins

Name	Source	Deficiencies	Maintenance	Light work	Medium work	Hard work	Pregnant and lactating mare	Growing horse
A (retinol)	Carrots. Carotene in green leafy plants. Cod liver oil. Stored in the liver and fat tissues.	Night blindness. Excessive tears. Rough coat. Lack of appetite. Poor blood cells. Infections of reproductive tract . Poor growth . Weak bones and tendons.	30 iu*/kg of bodyweight	30 iu/kg of bodyweight	45 iu/kg of bodyweight	45 iu/kg of bodyweight	60 iu/kg of bodyweight	45 iu/kg of bodyweight
D (calciferol)	D2 (ergocalciferol) Plants once cut and dried. D3 (cholecalciferol): Fish oils. Through the skin after contact with sunlight.	Reduced growth. Weak bones. Increased bone problems.	1,200 iu/kg of feed (dry matter)	1,250–1,300 iu/kg of feed (dry matter)	1,300–1,500 iu/kg of feed (dry matter)	1,500–2000 iu/kg of feed (dry matter)	2,000 iu/kg of feed (dry matter)	2,000 iu/kg of feed (dry matter)
E (tocopherol)	Leafy green forage. Good hay. Cereals. Alfalfa.	Anaemia. Swelling of joints. Muscular inco-ordination. White muscle disease. Yellowing of body fat. Reduced stamina.	50–80 iu/kg of dry matter	50–80 iu/kg of dry matter	50–80 iu/kg of dry matter	80–100 iu/kg of dry matter	100 iu/kg of dry matter	100 iu/kg of dry matter

Name	Source	Deficiencies	Maintenance	Light work	Medium work	Hard work	Pregnant and lactating mare	Growing horse
K	K (phylloquinone) Found in green leafy plants. Made in the hind gut by gut microflora (bacteria)	Longer clotting time of blood	No exact	figures	are	known		
		Haemorrhaging	No exact	figures	are	known		
	K2 (menaquinone) provided in supplements and converted in liver – menaquinone is common supplement used	"	"	"	"	"		

*iu = international unit

Table 2.7 Water-soluble vitamins: C

Name	Function	Requirements	Sources	Deficiencies and problems
C (ascorbic acid)	Essential for the formation of collagen tissue which is vital in tendons and cartilage. Essential for the utilisation of essential amino acids lysine and proline.	Not known. Supplementation has been known to assist in epistaxis (bleeding from the nose).	Made in the liver and other body cells.	No deficiencies have been recorded. Supplementation has been advisable in the following situations: when horse is sweating heavily or during periods of stress and growth.

Table 2.6 Water-soluble vitamins: B-complex

Name	Function	Requirements	Sources	Deficiencies and problems
B1 (thiamine)	Assists in metabolising carbohydrates. Maintains healthy nervous system. Assists in energy metabolism. Has been found to have a calming effect when fed to nervous horses. Can assist in the performance and stamina of competition horses.	Exact requirements are not known but 3–5 mg/kg dry matter should be sufficient.	Green forage Good hay Made by microflora in intestines Cereal grains Brewers yeast.	Dietary deficiencies are rare due to the vitamin being made in the intestines. Overfeeding is rare as most excesses are excreted in the urine within 24–36 hours. Certain plants such as bracken and horsetail cause thiamine to be destroyed so supplementation is essential if a horse has eaten these plants. Deficiencies can cause: – Weight loss – Muscular inco-ordination – Missed heart beats.
B2 (riboflavin)	Maintains healthy nervous system. Assists in energy metabolism.	No more than 2 milligrams per kg of dry matter per day.	Green forage Good hay Made by microflora in intestines Milk and milk products.	Dietary deficiency is very rare. Deficiencies can cause – Rough coat and dry skin – Conjunctivitis – Excessive tearing – Possibly connected with moon blindness. Overfeeding is rare as excesses are excreted in the urine within 24 hours.
B3 (niacin)	Metabolism of nutrients.	No specific requirements have been determined.	Green forage, especially Lucerne Oil seeds Made by microflora in intestines.	No deficiencies have been recorded in the horse and overfeeding is rare as most excesses are excreted in the urine within 24–36 hours. In humans a high level of niacin has resulted in dilation of blood vessels, sickness and itching skin.
B5 (pantothenic acid)	Assists in energy metabolism. Assists in the formation of antibodies.	No specific requirements have been determined.	Green forage Cereals and peas Made by microflora in intestines.	Dietary deficiency is very rare due to the vitamin being made by the microflora in the intestines.

Name	Function	Requirements	Sources	Deficiencies and problems
B6 (pyridoxine)	Assists in energy metabolism. Maintains health of the nervous system. Assists in formation of haemoglobin in the blood. Maintains health of immune system. Heavily worked horses have benefited from B6 supplementation.	No specific requirements have been determined.	Green forage Cereal grains Made by the microflora in the caecum and colon.	No deficiencies have been recorded in the horse and overfeeding is rare as most excesses are excreted in the urine within 24–36 hours.
B12 (cyanocobalamin)	Assists in the production of red blood cells. Assists in energy metabolism Fed to competition horses that are under stress. Can assist in putting on condition and correcting anaemia.	No specific requirements have been determined. Usually 4–10 micrograms per pound are fed when supplementation is required.	Made by the microflora in the caecum and colon. Green forages.	No deficiencies have been recorded in the horse and overfeeding is rare as most excesses are excreted in the urine within 24–36 hours. In other animals a high level of B12 has resulted in poor growth, weight loss, rough coat and increased nervousness.
B15 (pangamic acid)	Allegedly increases the supply of blood oxygen to the horse. No exact details provided to date.	No specific requirements have been determined.	Unknown.	No deficiencies have been recorded in the horse and overfeeding is rare as most excesses are excreted in the urine within 24–36 hours.
Biotin	Assists in the metabolism of energy Can assist in the improvement of poor quality hoof in some horses. Maintains sebaceous glands in skin. Maintains bone marrow.	10–30 milligrams daily for 6–9 months to improve hoof condition.	Made by the microflora in caecum. Yeast Green Forage Cereals.	No deficiencies have been recorded in the horse and overfeeding is rare as most excesses are excreted in the urine within 24–36 hours.
Choline	Assists in the transport of fats stored in the liver to other areas of the body for use as energy. Maintains a healthy nervous system.	If supplementation is required a dose of 500 milligrams is sufficient for a 500–600 kg horse.	Natural fats Green, leafy forage Yeast Cereals.	Deficiencies can lead to poor growth and increased storage of fats in the liver. Overfeeding is unknown as most excesses are excreted in the urine within 24–36 hours.
Folic acid	Assists cell metabolism. Required for red blood cell formation. Assists in general metabolism.	20 milligrams daily may be beneficial to stabled competition horses in hard work.	Green, leafy forage Made by the microflora in caecum.	No deficiencies have been recorded in the horse and overfeeding is rare as most excesses are excreted in the urine within 24–36 hours.

43

MINERALS

The horse requires a number of minerals which are divided into macrominerals and microminerals. All the minerals provided to the grazing horse are affected by the land that the horse grazes on as the plants receive their minerals from the soil and these are passed on to the horse. Should there be any deficiencies in the soil these will directly affect the grazing horse. However, the majority of horses are fed feeds that have been harvested from numerous places, which should balance any regional soil deficiencies. Compound mixes and cubes often have the macrominerals added, which also reduces the chances of deficiencies.

Healthy, mature horses are unlikely to require any additional mineral supplementation apart from that provided in the feeds. Horses that are growing and stud stock may require additional supplementation depending on their diet.

Table 2.8 Macrominerals

Name	Function	Sources	Deficiencies
Calcium (Ca)	Assists in contraction of muscles. Required for blood clotting. Assists in the production of hormones and enzymes. Works with phosphorous and vitamin D to produce bone. Approximately 35 per cent of bone is calcium. The ratio of calcium to phosphorous should be a minimum of 2:1 to ensure that adequate levels of calcium are absorbed during digestion.	Green, leafy forage Limestone Calcium gluconate Dicalcium Phosphate.	Rickets in young horses Developmental Orthopaedic Disease (DOD) Azoturia Poor muscle function Impaired blood clotting Joint problems and bone weakness.
Phosphorous (P)	Works in conjunction with calcium for bone growth. Assists in energy metabolism. Makes up approximately 15 per cent of bone. The ratio of calcium to phosphorous should be a minimum of 2:1. Too much phosphorous will reduce the absorption of any calcium fed during digestion.	Cereals Dicalcium Phosphate.	Overfeeding of phosphorous can lead to: – Lameness – Fragile bones – Enlargement of the jaw bone – Hyperparathyroidism (big head disease).
Magnesium (Mg)	Required for haemoglobin formation in the blood. Assists in bone formation. Assists in enzyme functions in the body.	Alfalfa Clover Bran Linseed Magnesium carbonate.	Deficiencies can lead to: – Nervousness and excitability – Increased respiratory rates – Muscle tremors – Aggressiveness and ill temper.
Sulphur (S)	Contains the amino acids methionine and cystine. Assists in enzyme and hormone production.	Protein feeds Green forage.	No deficiencies have been recorded but overdosing can lead to: – Loss of weight and appetite – Colic – A yellow, frothy discharge from the nostrils – Laboured breathing.
Sodium Chloride (NaCl)	Maintains the balance of fluids in the cells. Assists in muscle contractions. Removes waste products from the cells. Required in the production of bile (secreted from the liver during digestion). Maintains the health of the nervous system	Salt and salt licks Green forages, especially Alfalfa Electrolytes.	Deficiencies can lead to: – Dehydration – Poor growth – Reduced utilisation of energy – Muscle cramps Overfeeding can result in: – Dehydration – High blood pressure.
Potassium (K)	Works with sodium to assist in correct nerve function and muscular contractions. Assists in maintaining correct fluid balance in the body.	Green forage Molasses Electrolytes.	Deficiencies can lead to: – Weight loss – Diarrhoea – Muscle weakness.

Table 2.9 Macrominerals*

Name	Function	Sources	Deficiencies
Cobalt (Co)	A necessary part of vitamin B12. Assists in the activation of enzyme reactions.	Made by the microflora in the caecum and colon.	Deficiencies lead to a reduction of B12 production and, therefore, anaemia and reduced growth.
Zinc (Zn)	Assists in the metabolism of nutrients. Required for the immune system to function correctly. Required for healthy skin, hair and hooves. Assists in blood formation.	Yeast Bran Cereal germ Zinc sulphate	Deficiencies can lead to: – Dry, flaky skin – Hair loss – Poor growth rate.
Copper (Cu)	Works with sulphur and molybdenum. Essential in the formation of haemoglobin, cartilage and bone. Required for correct utilisation of iron in the body.	Grassland.	Deficiencies can lead to: – Brittle, weak bones – Anaemia – Faded dull coat – In foals, copper deficiency associated with osteochondritis.
Manganese (Mn)	Required for utilisation of carbohydrates and fats. Essential for the formation of cartilage. Assists in formation of bone. Assists in the formation of enzymes.	Wheat bran Grassland	Broodmares that become deficient can give birth to deformed foals whose bones are not correctly developed. Deficiency is rare as copper is readily available in grassland and hay and can be stored in the liver
Iron (Fe)	Essential for the formation of haemoglobin and red blood cells.	Grassland Cereals.	Deficiencies can lead to: – Anaemia – Poor performance – Poor growth in youngstock.

Name	Function	Sources	Deficiencies
Fluorine (F)	Essential for the formation of healthy teeth and bones. Assists in the prevention of tooth decay.	Pasture land and hay Water Limestone-based supplements.	Deficiencies are very rare as tap water has fluorine added to it. Overdosing (over 50 mg/kg) can occur if the soil and water have high levels of fluorine. The symptoms will be: – Discoloured, mottled weak teeth – Poor condition and rough coat – Lameness in joints.
Iodine (I)	Essential constituent of thyroxin needed for correct functioning of the thyroid gland. Required for reproductive cycle to function correctly.	Kelp Pasture land Mineral licks.	Broodmares deficient in iodine can exhibit abnormal oestrous cycles. Foals may be still-born, hairless or exhibit weakness and deformed joints. Overfeeding (5 mg/kg) can lead to enlarged thyroid glands, weakness and death of foals.
Selenium (Se)	Works with vitamin E. Essential part of antioxidant enzymes which help to remove toxins from the system. A component of the amino acids methionine and cystine. Assists in maintaining a healthy immune system.	Pasture land Alfalfa Brewers grains Linseed.	Deficiencies in foals can lead to: – Hair loss – Dark urine – Laboured breathing – White muscle disease. Deficiencies in any horse can lead to azoturia. Overfeeding (5 mg/kg) can cause poisoning.

These are required in very small amounts and overfeeding can lead to poisoning and in severe cases death.

Table 2.10 Daily mineral requirements of the horse

Name	Maintenance for 500kg horse	Working horses	Pregnant and lactating mares	Yearlings	2-year-olds
Calcium	25 g limestone 65 g	25-40 g limestone 65-105 g	33 g limestone 93 g	32 g limestone 88 g	28 g limestone 78 g
Phosphorous	19 g	18-29 g	26-28 g pregnant 22-36 g lactating	15-20 g	13 g
Magnesium	7-8 g	9-15 g	9 g pregnant 9-11 g lactating	5.5-9 g	7 g
Sulphur	0.15% of total diet	0.15% of total diet	0.15% of total diet	0.15% of total diet	0.15% of total diet
Sodium Chloride	0.1% of total diet (44g)	0.1% of total diet	0.1% of total diet	0.1% of total diet	0.1% of total diet
Potassium	25 g	31-50 g	29-31 g pregnant 33-46 g lactating	18 g	23 g
Cobalt	0.1 mg/kg*	0.1 mg/kg	0.1 mg/kg	0.1 mg/kg	0.1 mg/kg
Zinc	40 mg/kg	40 mg/kg	40 mg/kg	40 mg/kg	40 mg/kg
Copper	10 mg/kg	10 mg/kg	10 mg/kg	10 mg/kg	10 mg/kg
Manganese	40 mg/kg	40 mg/kg	40 mg/kg	40 mg/kg	40 mg/kg
Iron	40 mg/kg	40 mg/kg	50 mg/kg	50 mg/kg	50 mg/kg
Fluorine	0.1 mg/kg	0.1 mg/kg	0.1 mg/kg	0.1 mg/kg	0.1 mg/kg
Iodine	0.1 - 0.6 mg/kg	0.1 - 0.6 mg/kg	0.1 - 0.6 mg/kg	0.1 - 0.6 mg/kg	0.1 - 0.6 mg/kg
Selenium (estimated figures)	0.1 mg/kg	0.1 mg/kg	0.1 mg/kg	0.1 mg/kg	0.1 mg/kg

*mg/kg = milligrams per kilogram of total diet.
Adapted from Nutritional Requirements of Horses 5th Revised Edition (1989).

WATER

Horses can drink up to 15 gallons a day

We often forget about water when assessing the dietary requirements of the horse as it is usually freely available. Any consideration of the horse's diet should include some appreciation of the fluid content of the diet. Water is an essential nutrient and makes up 65–75 per cent of the weight of a horse.

Horses can live for up to twenty-five days without food but can only survive for a maximum of five days without water. A loss of 12–15 per cent of the body water can lead to severe dehydration and illness in the horse.

Use in the body

Water is necessary for all cell activities throughout the body and is present in all body fluids. It enables matter such as nutrients and waste to move in and out of all the cells in the body. The water in and around the cells is described as:

49

Extra-cellular fluid. This is water that is found outside the cells and in the bloodstream. The plasma usually contains 8 per cent water and there is generally 22 per cent around the cells in the tissues of the body.

Intracellular fluid. This is the water found inside the cell and makes up approximately 70 per cent of the total water in the body.

Water plays many other functions in the body as listed below:

- Controls and regulates body temperature, evaporating in sweat.
- Is essential for the life and shape of all cells.
- Is a constituent of lymph in the lymphatic system.
- Produces saliva, which is an essential part of the digestive process.
- Transports nutrients and waste products between the cells.
- Acts as a base for urine and faeces, enabling waste to be excreted.
- Lubricates the joints and is a constituent of the synovial fluid found in joints.
- Provides a fluid cushion to protect the nervous system.
- Provides a fluid bag to protect the foetus in a pregnant mare.
- Makes up 91 per cent of a mare's milk.
- Transports sound waves in a fluid found in the ear.
- Lubricates and cleans the eyes.

Requirements

Every horse requires a constant supply of fresh water in order to stay healthy and enable all the systems to function correctly.

Certain factors can increase the horse's demand for water. These include:

- Age – young horses have a higher requirement for water.
- Activity – the harder a horse works the more water it will require.
- Pregnancy – mares also have higher water requirements.
- Temperature – hot humid conditions increase the horse's water requirements.
- Type of feed – horses fed dry hay and dry concentrates will have a greater water requirement.

Table 2.11 Water requirement in a 600 kg horse in 60–70 degrees F

Activity	Gallons per day
Maintenance	5–8
Medium work	9–15
Hard work	12–15+
Pregnancy	8–9
Lactation	9–11

Providing water in the stable

There are numerous ways of supplying water to a horse but in all cases it is essential that the water is kept clean and fresh, is not contaminated and is easily accessible to the horse. The type of system chosen for in the stable is dependent on the layout of the stables, available funds and personal preference. The two common systems used are discussed below.

Buckets
Plastic or rubber buckets can be used to supply water. They should be large (3–5 gallons) and be changed at least twice a day, even if not empty, as the water becomes stale and dirty. Ideally the buckets should be kept off the floor by hanging them at shoulder height. This reduces the risk of buckets being kicked over or becoming full of bedding. If they are kept on the floor the handle should be turned away from the horse to prevent them catching it. When changing the buckets they must be washed out and cleaned before refilling.

The advantage of using buckets is that the water intake of each horse can be easily checked but it is time-consuming and labour-intensive. It also hold the risk of a horse running out of water and becoming dehydrated as the supply is dependent on the owner.

Automatic water systems
These are popular due to the labour-saving aspect and the fact that the horse has a constant, fresh supply of water available. This does not mean they can be left unchecked! The bowl should be checked at least twice a day as it can become contaminated with food or muck and the system can stop working, so leaving the horse without water until fixed. The bowls should be thoroughly cleaned out regularly to keep the water clean. They must be large enough for a horse to fit his muzzle in with ease and should be fixed at shoulder height. During the winter the pipes need to be lagged to stop them freezing up and also need to be protected from inquisitive horses!

The disadvantages are that unless you have a gauge attached to the system it can be difficult to tell how much water is being consumed and some horses do not like using them. They are also expensive to install and are prone to clogging or damage by bored horses!

Providing water in the field

Water supplied in fields is often shared by a number of horses or other animals and is subject to contamination from the other horses, insects, vermin, algae, leaves, etc. Water systems can be either natural, such as streams or springs, or by provision of the owner by troughs or buckets. The most common systems are:

Streams and rivers

A fresh, unpolluted stream or river is an excellent source of water. Unfortunately the majority of streams are polluted and should be fenced off. If you are lucky enough to have a fresh water stream in the field it needs to have a stony, firm bottom and be deep enough to provide enough clean water for the horse. Any streams or rivers with a sandy base must not be used as they can lead to sand colic.

The advantage of a stream or river is that there is a constant supply available, they rarely freeze or dry up and they need minimal maintenance.

Water troughs

There are two types of trough used: self-filling with a ballcock system and troughs that need to be filled by the owner. The self-filling troughs have the advantage of providing a constant supply of fresh water but can be broken by inquisitive horses.

Any trough must be safe. The standard dimension is 1–2 metres long and 0.5 metres deep. There should be no sharp edges or dangerous protrusions and it should be raised about 23 cm above the ground.

All troughs need to be cleaned out regularly especially after the autumn when they can become full of leaves. They need to be checked daily and kept clean.

The trough needs to be located in an area that is accessible for all the horses and will not become too poached. The ideal place is away from trees and shrubs, and along a fence line rather than in a corner where a horse can be trapped by others while drinking.

Care needs to be taken if using a trough for young foals as there have been incidents of foals falling in and drowning. Bars placed over the top of the trough can minimise this risk.

Problems

If a horse does not receive a regular supply of fresh, clean water it will suffer from dehydration. The level of dehydration will be dependent on the work the horse is doing, the weather conditions and how little has been drunk. Ill horses can become dehydrated if they are off food and water or have a bout of diarrhoea. Only 3 per cent needs to be lost for dehydration to occur and a loss of 12–15 per cent can be fatal.

Signs that a horse is becoming dehydrated are:

- The skin pinch test. A piece of skin is pinched on the neck. In the healthy horse this should spring back immediately. If the skin remains raised for over two seconds the horse is suffering dehydration. Should it remain raised for more than five seconds the dehydration is severe.
- The blood becomes more concentrated.
- The horse will look tucked up.

- The urine will be dark in colour and reduced in amount.
- The skin can look dry and tight and the horse may perform below par.

If dehydration is not caught early or the horse is not drinking correctly, the body will begin to draw fluid from other areas. Initially water is taken from the gut, which will affect digestion and can lead to colic and blockages. Once this has been depleted water is taken from the cells and blood. This can lead to muscle damage and in severe cases brain damage.

The most common method of correcting mild dehydration is to:

- Ensure they have a constant supply of fresh water.
- Feed wet feeds such as sloppy sugarbeet and wet hay.
- Feed electrolytes. These can be bought as powders and are mixed into the feed or water. They contain a variety of trace minerals such as sodium, chloride and potassium and help address the imbalance of fluids and encourage the horse to drink (electrolytes are discussed in detail in Chapter 10).

Rules of watering

In order to minimise the problems associated with providing water for horses a list of rules has been devised and is given below:

- A constant supply of fresh, clean water should always be available.
- If buckets are used to provide a constant supply of water they must be changed and cleaned out at least twice a day and topped up as necessary.
- If water cannot be left with the horse it must be offered at least six times a day and always before feeding.
- Water a hot horse with lukewarm water so as not to shock the system.
- If a horse has been deprived of water or has been working hard it should only be given small quantities of water at frequent intervals to quench the thirst and only offered a bucketful once fully recovered.
- During hunting or endurance rides when the horse is out for many hours he should be offered water at various times throughout the day to prevent dehydration.
- If a horse has access to a constant supply of fresh water there is no need to take the water away prior to work or feeding.

ASSESSMENT OF YOUR HORSE'S NUTRIENT REQUIREMENTS

This work sheet is designed to enable you to easily assess your own horse's nutrient requirements.

Name of your horse: ....

Date: ....

Age of the horse: ....

Height: ....

1. Health of your horse: grade the health of your horse by selecting the relevant grade.

	Grading	Your horse's grade
Excellent health	5	
Good health	4	
Suffers from respiratory problems	3	
Poor health	2	
Ill or convalescing	1	

2. Condition of your horse Using Table 1.1 on page 16, condition score your horse and fill in the grade below.

Available score	Optimum score for particular disciplines	Your horse's score
1 Poor condition	Dressage: 6–7	
2 Very thin	Eventers: 4–5	
3 Thin	Showjumpers: 5–6	
4 Moderately thin	Broodmares 5–6	
5 Moderate	Show hacks 6–7	
6 Fleshy		
7 Fat		
8 Over fat		

54

3. Your horse's age Grade your horse on the chart below in relation to its age.

Age	Grade	Your horse's score
1–3	1	
4–6	2	
6–10	3	
10–15	3	
15 and over	2	

4. Temperament and breed Select the description that best suits your horse and write the score in the adjacent box.

Description	Score	Your score
Warmblood type with lazy temperament	4	
Warmblood type with good temperament	3	
Warmblood type with sharp temperament	2	
Native x Thoroughbred and lazy	4	
Native x Thoroughbred and sharp	2	
Native with lazy temperament	3	
Native with good temperament	2	
Native with sharp temperament	2	
Thoroughbred with fretful temperament	3	
Thoroughbred with good temperament	3	
Arab x with fretful temperament	2	
Arab x with good temperament	3	
Arab x with lazy temperament	4	
Arab with sharp temperament	2	
Arab with good temperament	3	
Arab with fretful temperament	2	

5. Nutrient demands Circle the relevant number that fits your horse's nutrient demands for each nutrient listed.

Nutrient		Score: 5 = high demand 1 = low demand				
Simple Carbohydrates: quick release energy		1	2	3	4	5
Complex Carbohydrates: slow release energy		1	2	3	4	5
Protein: growth, repair and renewal	Your horse's crude protein level in % (from table 2.3)	1	2	3	4	5
Fats: energy		1	2	3	4	5
Vitamins and minerals		1	2	3	4	5
Water		1	2	3	4	5

If your horse has a high score of 4 or 5 it means they have a high demand for nutrients. If the number is mid-way (3), they have a moderate demand and if the figure is low (1–2) they have a low demand.

These scores will be used later when designing a diet for your horse.

CHAPTER 3

Feeds and their Nutritional Value

Having gained an understanding of the nutritional requirements of your horse, the next step is to understand what you are actually feeding to your horse and if it is providing the necessary nutrients.

CHOOSING YOUR FEED

Horses' feed has changed very little over the years. Even during Roman times the horse's diet was a variety of cereal grains and hay. In fact the diet for the Roman cavalry horse was very similar to that of today's horse.

The most common grain fed was barley, which had a higher energy value than the barley used today, and each cavalry horse was allocated 1.5 kg of grain per day. The most common hay fed was lucerne (alfalfa), which the Romans called *Medica*. This lucerne was combined with clover and a variety of herbs including fenugreek and vetch. Beans and peas were fed to improve condition and they even made their own coarse mixes!

An example of a Roman coarse mix fed to racehorses consisted of: three measures of barley, six measures of horse beans, six measures of wheat, eight measures of chick-peas and cooked kidney beans, four measures of vetch and three measures of fenugreek. This was all mixed up with a pint of sparrow egg yolks and alfalfa chaff. It was no doubt a very nutritious feed!

When deciding what to feed today's horse, certain factors need to be considered such as:

- Your horse's specific requirements – as discussed in Chapter 2.
- How many horses you intend to feed – grains have a shorter shelf life than compound feeds so will need to be used more quickly.
- The cost of the feeds – compound feeds are generally more expensive.
- The quality of the feeds – you must only feed good quality feeds.
- Storage available – can you buy in bulk and will it get used before the sell-by date? Is the storage dry and vermin-proof?

Having considered these factors, you then need to know what selection of feeds are available to fulfil these requirements, and there is certainly no shortage of choice!

The rest of the chapter will discuss the feed values of the common concentrate and roughage feeds and the type of horse that would be suited to such feeds.

CONCENTRATE FEEDS

This is the energy-providing part of the feed and has been traditionally provided through cereals such as oats and barley. The reason why these feeds were called concentrates is that they are a more concentrated form of energy. For example, 1 kg of barley has an energy value of 13 MJDE, and 1 kg of average hay contains 8 MJDE so you could replace 1.5 kg of hay with 1 kg of barley but still provide the same level of energy, hence the name *concentrate*.

When a horse is not in work or in very light work they can usually receive all the energy they require from the roughage part of the diet and do not really require any additional energy from concentrate feeds. As the workload increases this roughage will not contain enough energy and the horse may begin to lose weight and performance may suffer. This is when concentrate feeds have their use. You can top up the horse's roughage diet with concentrates to provide the correct level of energy for the horse to work and perform to the best of their ability.

THE CARBOHYDRATE-RICH CONCENTRATE FEEDS

Oats

Description
Oats are one of the traditional grain feeds that are often fed to horses in fast work and have been fed as the complete concentrate ration. This is because they are easily available, being harvested on many farms, have a good fibre content and low energy content, despite the 'heating effect' (see page 59).

Oats can be very variable in quality and it is important to feed only those of high quality. A good oat should be plump, cleaned and bright in colour. Ideally there should be a high proportion of kernel (the inner part of the oat containing the nutrients) to hull (the outer fibrous coat) as these oats will be more nutritious. The heavier the oat the higher the nutritional value.

Oats can be fed whole to horses over the age of one year but they require extra chewing so it is more common to feed them bruised, rolled or crushed. These processes crack open the outer hull and thus reduce the amount of chewing needed and increase digestibility. The problem with opening up the hulls is that the oats lose their nutritional value more quickly.

Naked oats

A modern development of oats has been the naked oat. As its name suggests the outer hull has been removed leaving just the kernels. This makes them higher in energy per kg and less fibrous. They do not require any processing as there is no hull to crack open and as they are more dense in weight less needs to be fed to the horse.

Table 3.1 Nutritional value: oats

	MJDE/kg	Crude protein %	Lysine %	Calcium %	Phosphorous %
Oats	11–12	10	0.44	0.05	0.34
Naked oats	16	13.5	0.5	0.2	0.4

Storage

Rolled oats should be used within two to three weeks of rolling if they are to maintain their feed value. Whole oats should last for several months if stored in a dry, vermin-proof container.

Problems

Some owners are wary of feeding oats due to their apparent heating effect. In fact oats are one of the lower energy grains containing a similar energy content to some of the 'cooling' or 'non-heating' mixes available! The bad name gained by the oat can come from two sources:

FERMENTATION. When the correct amount of oats are fed to a horse they are digested in the small intestine and the energy passes into the bloodstream and is used by the body. If too many oats are fed or if the horse does not digest the oats properly some oats may not be dealt with in the small intestine and get passed into the large intestine. They should not really be here as the large intestine is designed to deal only with complex carbohydrates. These stray oats get rapidly fermented by the intestinal microflora. This fermentation results in a surge of glucose and volatile fatty acids pouring into the bloodstream causing a surge of energy making the horse 'hot up'.

OVERFEEDING. Many horses that apparently 'hot up' are simply getting too much energy in their diet. They are gaining a high level of energy from an incorrect diet and may not be getting enough exercise to use such energy and so have to release this excess somehow, which tends not to be in a constructive way!

CALCIUM/PHOSPHOROUS. The other main problem associated with any grain is that the calcium/phosphorous ratio is not correct. There can be too much phosphorous, meaning that the grain ration needs to be balanced by the addition of a calcium supplement or the addition of a rich calcium feed such as sugarbeet or limestone.

Barley

Description
Barley is another popular grain fed to horses. It has a higher energy content than oats but has a lower protein and lysine content. It is a heavier grain with a lower percentage of hull to kernel making it denser in energy and easier to overfeed. Barley has traditionally been fed as a conditioning feed as, due to the energy content, it puts weight on horses.

The hull of barley is very tough and is too strong to be digested by the horse, thus it can only be fed if processed. The common forms fed are rolled, crushed or cooked. Cooking barley gelatinises the starch making it more digestible to the horse. The common cooking methods used are boiling, micronisation or extrusion. As with oats you must only feed high-quality barley which is clean, heavy and plump.

Brewer's grains
Barley may also be fed to horses in the form of brewer's yeast and dried brewer's grains, which are used as supplements in the diet. There has been recent research into the nutritional benefits of feeding brewer's grains and malt distiller's grains to horses. So far the results have shown these by-products of the brewing and distilling industries were palatable, assisted in the weight gain of horses and provided a nutritional supplement to the diet.

Table 3.2 Nutritional value: barley

MJDE/kg	Crude protein %	Lysine %	Calcium %	Phosphorous %
13	9.5	0.40	0.05	0.34

Barley is a rich source of the B vitamin niacin.

Storage
As with oats, rolled or crushed barley needs to be used within two or three weeks. Boiled barley must be used immediately. The processed forms such as micronised flaked barley or extruded barley will have the sell-by date printed on the sacks and this should be checked before purchase.

Problems
Some horses can have an allergic reaction to barley which results in lumps appearing under the skin and the lower legs becoming filled. If this occurs barley should be removed from the ration.

Maize (corn)

Description
Maize is a high energy grain that can, like oats, have a 'heating effect' on the horse. Known as corn in the USA, it contains twice the digestible energy of oats. The grain is very hard and so tends to be fed cracked, rolled or cooked. Cooking maize reduces its heating effect as this stops the starch from being fermented. Due to the high energy, low fibre content of maize it tends to make up no more that 25 per cent of a ration.

A good sample of maize should be clean, bright yellow in colour, plump and firm. It is essential that any maize fed is free from moulds as they can cause liver damage, brain damage and possibly death in the horse.

Table 3.3 Nutritional value: maize

MJDE/kg	Crude protein %	Lysine %	Calcium %	Phosphorous %
14	9.1	0.25	0.05	0.27

Maize is the only grain that contains carotene, a precursor of vitamin A.

Storage
Whole maize can last for several months if stored in dry conditions. Once cracked or crushed it needs to be used within three weeks.

Problems
Maize is high in energy so can lead to weight gain and digestive disorders. As discussed earlier with oats, fermentation and overfeeding can occur, which will lead to horses hotting up. It is known as a low quality protein feed as it is lacking in lysine and other essential amino acids and this can lead to growth problems in youngstock if other high quality protein feeds are not mixed into the ration.

Wheat

Description
Wheat grain is not a common feed in the UK but is commonly used in the USA. Due to the extensive use of wheat in the human food chain it is a relatively expensive grain. The grains are free from a hull and small in size and so can miss being properly chewed. This risk can be reduced if the grain is cracked or steam flaked. The steaming also increases the digestibility of the grain.

Wheat by-products
The milling process leads to a number of by-products being available: wheat germ, bran and middlings. Germ is very expensive to feed to horses, the middlings tend to be very dusty and of a poor nutritional value, but the bran is a common feed used in horse diets.

Wheat bran has been used traditionally as a bulking agent to increase the size and fibre content of a feed. Bran actually contains less fibre than oats and much of the fibre content is made of lignin, which is very hard to digest. Good quality bran should have large, dust-free flakes and be fed only as a supplement to any feed. The most common use of bran is as a laxative. It has the ability to absorb a vast amount of water which gives it a laxative effect on the intestines.

Table 3.4 Nutritional value: wheat

	MJDE/kg	Crude protein %	Lysine %	Calcium %	Phosphorous %
Wheat grain	11	11	0.34	0.03	0.36
Wheat bran	11	15	0.56	0.13	1.13

Storage
Wheat bran needs to be stored in a dry environment as any dampness will be absorbed and make it musty.

Problems
Wheat should never be fed ground as its gluten content makes it gluey and it can become a doughy lump in the stomach leading to colic. Wheat bran has a very high level of phosphorous causing a large imbalance in the calcium and phosphorous ratio. Therefore it must be fed with a calcium-rich supplement to prevent any bone problems occurring.

Sugarbeet pulp

Description
Sugarbeet pulp is a very good source of simple carbohydrates, calcium and fibre. Traditionally it was used as a supplement to tempt horses to eat or to damp down feeds. But in fact there is a lot more to sugarbeet than just a sweet addition to a feed.

The energy content of sugarbeet is very close to that of oats and it is very rich in calcium so does not pose any risk to the calcium/phosphorous ratio of a diet. The sugar content of the beet is used by the horse as 'instant energy' and the fibre content can be fermented in the hind gut and used as a form of slower release energy. This dual aspect means the feed can benefit a whole variety of horses.

The water content is an added benefit. Very wet sugarbeet can be used to rehydrate horses who are not drinking and can help encourage endurance horses to drink during a ride.

When adding sugarbeet to a diet it should be calculated and weighted as *dry* and then have the water added to it in order for the horse to benefit from the energy and fibre content and not just the weight of the water. Horses can be fed up to 1 kg a day *dry weight* (which will swell to between 2–2.5 kg once soaked) without causing digestive upsets.

Sugarbeet is a useful feed for endurance horses, hunters, horses that drop weight, youngsters and any horse that needs to put on weight and condition.

Soaking

When using traditional sugarbeet it is essential that it is soaked as it absorbs a vast amount of water and swells up. Shreds need to be soaked for approximately 12 hours, and pellets need 24 hours.

There is now a form of extruded sugarbeet available that has already been soaked and then dried so does not require soaking prior to feeding. This can be fed dry but is better fed with some water otherwise it defeats the object of feeding a wet feed.

Make sure you do not get the two types of sugarbeet mixed up and if in doubt soak it anyway!

Table 3.5 Nutritional value: sugarbeet

MJDE/kg	Crude protein %	Lysine %	Calcium %	Phosphorous %
10	8	0.5	0.62	0.09

Storage

Sugarbeet pellets or shreds must be stored in a dry environment as they absorb moisture and will turn mouldy. Once soaked, sugarbeet should be used within 24 hours as it goes off rapidly, especially in the summer.

Problems

Some horses suffer diarrhoea if fed too much sugarbeet. If you feed standard sugarbeet dry it can cause dehydration and colic.

CONCENTRATES HIGH IN PROTEIN

Linseed

Description

Linseed is the seed of the flax plant and is a good source of protein. It is used as a supplement to the feed as it is extremely rich in protein and can have a laxative effect. It is an excellent addition to the feed of poor horses, thin horses or if you wish to improve the condition of your horse's coat.

The seeds are small, shiny and brown with tough outer shells. When raw these seeds are poisonous to the horse. If fed uncooked they will release a chemical called hydrocyanic acid which causes cyanide poisoning and will kill the horse.

When cooking linseed the seeds should be soaked for 24 hours to soften them and then brought to the boil and simmered until all the seeds have cracked and the linseed has become a jelly. If you do not wish to go through this laborious cooking process you can buy linseed that is already processed and safe to feed. The common forms are linseed cake, linseed meal and linseed oil.

Linseed can be very beneficial to horses suffering from respiratory problems as it has a soothing effect on the respiratory tract.

Table 3.6 Nutritional value: linseed meal

MJDE/kg	Crude protein %	Lysine %	Calcium %	Phosphorous %
18.5	30	1.16	0.3	0.8

Problems
As mentioned earlier, linseed is very poisonous if fed raw. It can also be a laxative so should not be fed more than three times a week.

Peas and beans

Description
Field peas and beans have been added to the feed for many years to improve protein content. They are a valuable source of the essential amino acid lysine and have a good energy value, making them a useful addition to the diet of youngstock or competition horses in hard work.

Any field peas or beans fed must be clean and free from moulds. Beans are usually cracked or ground but can be fed whole to horses with sound teeth.

Table 3.7 Nutritional value: field beans

MJDE/kg	Crude protein %	Lysine g/kg	Calcium g/kg	Phosphorous g/kg
14	23	15.8	0.7	4.0

Problems
If you use any other beans check that they are safe to feed as many such as kidney beans require cooking prior to feeding as they can be toxic if fed raw. Field peas and beans are very high in phosphorous and low in calcium so must be fed with a calcium supplement.

Soyabeans

Description

Soyabeans are the most common protein supplement fed to horses. They are very rich in protein and also contain high levels of the essential amino acids, making them a high quality protein feed.

Raw soyabeans are toxic if fed and must be cooked to destroy any poisonous elements. Cooking does not affect the protein content of the feed. The common forms fed are soyabean meal, soya oil and soyabean flakes (usually found in mixes).

Soya is a valuable addition to the feed of any horse that needs the protein level topped up. Soyameal fed to broodmares during lactation has been found to improve the growth rate and condition of the suckling foals.

Table 3.8 Nutritional value: soyabean meal

MJDE/kg	Crude protein %	Lysine %	Calcium %	Phosphorous %
13	44	2.87	0.35	0.63

Soyabean meal is a rich source of lysine.

Problems

Soyabean must not be fed to horses when whole and raw as it is toxic and will cause digestive disturbances. As soya is so rich in protein it should only be used as a supplement. Too much protein fed in the diet can lead to digestive problems such as colic and metabolic problems such as lumps appearing under the skin.

Milk by-products

Description

Milk is an excellent source of lysine and the minerals calcium and phosphorous. Most horses also find milk very palatable and it can be a useful addition to the diet of a poor horse or a horse that is off its feed. The common by-products fed to horses are milk pellets and milk powder.

Table 3.9 Nutritional value: milk by-products

	MJDE/kg	Crude protein %	Lysine g/kg	Calcium g/kg	Phosphorous g/kg
Skimmed powder	18	36	Not available	N/A	N/A
Milk pellets	18	36	N/A	N/A	N/A

Problems

Adult horses may suffer diarrhoea and digestive upsets if fed milk products as they lack the enzyme lactase which is needed to digest milk sugars.

CONCENTRATES HIGH IN FAT

Vegetable oils

Description

Oil can be a useful addition to the diet of hard-working horses who require a high energy diet. It is a very concentrated form of energy, providing twice the amount of energy as the same potion of oats. This means that by adding oil to the diet a horse can be fed the required energy without too much bulk, so reducing the problems of overfeeding and the horse going off its feed.

Oil can help improve condition on thin or poor horses and has been shown to assist the growth of foals when fed to the lactating broodmare. Endurance riders have been adding oil to the diet of their horses as it provides a high level of slow release energy and can improve stamina and endurance.

The most common vegetable oils fed are sunflower oil and corn oil.

Table 3.10 Nutritional value: vegetable oil

	MJDE/kg	Crude protein %	Lysine %	Calcium %	Phosphorous %
Vegetable oil	35	0	0	0	0

Storage

Oils need to be kept out of direct sunlight and in a cool environment to prevent the oil becoming rancid.

Problems

Overfeeding oil (more than 12 per cent of the diet) can lead to diarrhoea and metabolic problems.

Table 3.11 Concentrates: summary of carbohydrate feeds

Feed	Energy content MJDE/kg	Protein content CP%	Calcium/ Phosphorous ratio	Types of horse that may benefit from feed	Problems with feed
Oats	11–12	10	Poor	Competition horses. Youngstock.	Must be fed with a calcium supplement. Can make horses hot up.
Naked oats	16	13	Poor	Horses in medium –hard work. Stud stock. Race Horses.	Must be fed with a calcium supplement. Can make horses hot up.
Barley	13	9.5	Poor	Competition horses. Horses that need to put on condition and weight.	Can put on too much weight May have allergic reaction.
Maize	14	9.1	Poor	Horses in medium –hard work.	Can make horses hot up. Can cause growth problems in youngstock.
Wheat-bran	11	15	Poor	For horses who need laxative. As a base to feed medicines. For ill/tired horses who cannot cope with a rich feed.	Can cause constipation if fed dry. Very poor calcium content which can lead to bone problems.
Sugarbeet	10	8	Good	Competition horses. Endurance horses. Ill/tired horses. Youngstock.	Can cause diarrhoea if too much fed. Never to be fed dry unless extruded.

Table 3.12 Concentrates: summary of protein feeds

Feed	Energy content MJDE/kg	Protein content CP %	Calcium/ Phosphorous ratio	Types of horse that may benefit from feed	Problems with feed
Linseed	18.5	30	Poor	Youngstock. Competition horses. Show horses. Horses that need to put on condition.	Poisonous if fed raw. Can cause diarrhoea if fed too frequently.
Peas and beans	14	23	Very poor	Competition horses in hard work. Broodmares and stud stock.	Ensure you feed with a calcium supplement.
Soyabean meal	13	44	Poor	Competition horses in hard work. Stud stock. Lactating broodmares.	Ensure you feed with a calcium supplement. Do not feed raw.
Milk powder	18	36	Good	Youngstock. Horses that need to put on condition.	Can cause diarrhoea if overfed.

Table 3.13 Concentrates: summary of fat concentrates

Feed	Energy content MJDE/kg	Protein content CP %	Calcium/ Phosphorous ratio	Types of horse that may benefit from feed	Problems with feed
Vegetable oil and corn oil	35	0	None	Broodmares: when conceiving and lactating. Youngstock. Competition horses in hard work. Endurance horses.	Can cause horses to put on too much weight. If too much is fed (over 12% of diet) can lead to diarrhoea.

COMPOUND FEEDS

The title compound feeds covers all the mixes and cubes manufactured by the feed companies. Horse owners have often made their own mixes up but the ingredients were often chosen for their individual qualities and the nutritional balance of each ingredient was unknown or taken for granted.

Commercially prepared mixes and cubes have the great advantage of being nutritionally balanced. The feed companies employ nutritionists who determine the feed ingredients, ensure all the individual nutrients balance and devise feed programmes for the feeds. There are now a vast range of compound feeds available and most disciplines and horse types are covered.

Concentrate cubes

Description
These pellets are made from a mixture of ingredients that are blended together with a binding agent such as molasses. They are often passed through steam for cooking and are finally forced through a die under pressure to form a pellet. Cubes manufactured for horses come in a range of sizes from 3 millimetres to 12 millimetres. Smaller pellets can take longer to eat and cause fewer problems with bolting whereas large pellets need more thorough chewing.

Cubes are often cheaper than mixes but some owners do not like to feed them as they cannot see the ingredients. Cubes are also heavier in weight than coarse mixes and so fewer need to be fed to provide the same energy levels.

Advantage of cubes
They are nutritionally balanced.
The quality of ingredients is guaranteed by reputable manufacturers.
Cubes have a longer shelf life than cereals.
They are easy and quick to feed.
They are easy to store.
They are dust-free.
They can be more cost effective when feeding a number of horses.
The nutritional value is stated on the sack so you know exactly what you are feeding.

Disadvantages
Older horses or those with teeth problems can find them difficult to eat.
They can be very dry if fed alone.
It is difficult to add in powders and medicines.
Some owners find them boring to feed.

Coarse mixtures

Description
These were produced to solve the problem of not being able to see what was being fed. The ingredients used are identical to cubes but are not bound up in pellets. The cereals used are usually processed by micronising, flaking and rolling and then mixed with molasses or other sugar-rich additives.

Advantage of coarse mixtures
They are nutritionally balanced.
You can assess the ingredients to ascertain the energy value.
They are lighter in weight than cubes so more can be fed which can be useful when horses are on small rations.
The feed is softer to eat than cubes.
Like cubes, they have a consistent level of nutrients and quality of ingredients.
The feed is dust-free.
The nutritional value is stated on the sack so you know exactly what is being fed.

Disadvantages of coarse mixtures
Horses can be fussy and pick out the ingredients they like leaving the ingredients they dislike, leading to wastage.
They have a shorter shelf life than cubes due to the higher moisture content.

Extruded feeds

Description
Extruded feeds such as barley and sugarbeet have been cooked in steam with temperatures in excess of 100 degrees centigrade, the feed is then dried and pelleted. The pellets are less dense and more bulky than conventional cubes. The extrusion process makes the feed easier to digest and often minerals and vitamins are added to make the feeds nutritionally balanced.

Advantages of extruded feeds
The cooking process makes the feed more digestible so reducing the risk of digestive disorders such as azoturia.
Extruded feeds are apparently utilised more effectively in the horse's digestive system, therefore the horse receives the same nutrients from less feed, making it more cost-effective.
They usually have a longer shelf life than mixes due to containing less moisture.
You can feed less feed to supply the same level of energy as oats or mixes.
The feed is dust-free.
The nutritional value is stated on the sack so you know exactly what is being fed.

Disadvantages of extruded feeds
They can be very dry if no succulent feeds or water is added.
Due to the increased digestibility owners can feed too much in each feed leading to overweight horses.

Complete cubes

Description
These cubes are designed to provide everything to the horse, hay and concentrates all in one !

Advantages
They are nutritionally balanced and the nutritional content is stated on the sack. These cubes have a high fibre content and contain all the required minerals and vitamins so can be very useful for native ponies or horses living out at grass who need a little extra.
The cubes can be a useful alternative to hay or haylage when a dust-free diet is required

Disadvantages
Horses fed complete cubes and given no hay or other roughage can develop stable vices such as cribbing due to boredom and a lack of long fibre to chew on.
They can develop digestive disorders such as colic if fibre is not sufficient.

Feed balancers

Description
Balancing cubes or mixes are designed to be fed with a cereal, usually oats, and when combined provide a balanced diet. Balancers contain a high level of protein and higher levels of minerals and vitamins, which compensates for the deficiencies in cereal grains. The ratio of cereals to balancer are stated on the sack.

Advantages
This system provides more freedom to alter individual diets according to the level of work done.
The combining of compound feeds and cereals allows the owner to alter the energy levels as applicable using the cereals but still keep the diet nutritionally balanced.

Disadvantages
The mixing of cereals and balancer needs careful weighing and correct feeding in order to achieve a balanced diet.
This is more time-consuming and can be complicated.

Nutritional value of compound feeds
Every manufacturer provides a vast variety of cubes and mixes for horses and each one is slightly different. Although the nutritional value of each manufacturer's feeds will be slightly different the ingredients tend to be very similar.

71

Common ingredients used in compound feeds are:

Alfalfa	source of fibre and protein
Soyabean	source of protein
Peas and beans	source of protein
Wheat	source of energy
Maize	source of energy
Barley	source of energy
Locust bean	source of energy and protein
Oat straw	source of fibre
Grass pellets	source of fibre
Sugarbeet pulp	source of energy and fibre, sweetens feed
Linseed cake	source of protein
Sunflower pellets	source of protein and fibre.
Dicalcium phosphate	source of calcium and phosphorous
Variety of herbs	for interest and vitamin and mineral content.

The only way to ascertain the exact nutritional value of a specific sack of compound feed is to read the label or the manufacturers' literature which will list the nutrient levels.

The following tables list the more common compound feeds manufactured and states their nutritional value but it is by no means a definitive list!

The general trend for compound feeds is that low energy feeds have a high fibre content and as energy increases the fibre content decreases. The protein content tends not to alter to dramatically, ranging from 10–12 per cent.

The tables reveal quite a variety of nutritional values in the range of manufacturers' feeds available. Though initially daunting, having searched through all the values it does enable the owner to pick a feed that suits their individual horse's requirements.

Table 3.14 Low energy mixes and cubes

Feed	Energy MJDE/kg	Protein content CP %	Oil % (Energy)	Fibre content CP %	Manufacturers' feed recommendations
Allen & Page quiet mix	9	10	2.5	14	Oat-free mix, specifically designed for horses and ponies in light work or at rest.
Allen and Page Quiet pencils	8.5	10	2.75	16	Oat-free cubes for horses and ponies.
Badminton Horse and pony cubes	8.75	11	3	14	A non-heating feed which provides the horse or pony in light work with a careful balance of protein and energy to avoid hotting up.
Badminton Four star cubes	9.5	11.5	3.75	14	Cubes designed for feeding to horses and ponies in moderate work. Ideal for horses or ponies who need energy without fizz.
Baileys No 9 all–rounder	11	10.5	3	14	A coarse mix formulated for riding horses and ponies in light and moderated work.
Baileys Horse and pony cubes	10	11.5	2.5	16	A non-heating, fully balanced feedstuff designed to meet the concentrate requirement of horses and ponies at rest or in light work.
Balanced Horse Feeds Oatless mix	8.5	9	4	11	An oatless mix especially formulated for horses and ponies that hot up on cereal mixes containing oats.
Balanced Horse Feeds Cool cubes	9.5	10.5	3.8	16	A high fibre cube formulated especially for ponies and horses on a maintenance diet.
Burgess and Sneyd Supabarley	13	10.5	4.5	4.5	A non-heating, extrusion-cooked complete horse feed.
Dodson & Horrell Pasture mix	10	9.5	3.25	12.7	An oat-free mix especially formulated to meet nutrient requirement of ponies and non-competitive leisure horses.
Spillers Horse and pony cubes	10.1	10.5	3	14	A low energy, non-heating palatable feed ideal for all horses and ponies in general work.
Spillers Cool mix	11.5	11	2.5	11.5	The lowest energy mix in the Spillers range. An oat-free mix suitable for all horses and ponies in light to moderate work.

Table 3.15 Herbal quiet mixes and cubes

Feed	Energy MJDE/kg	Protein content CP%	Oil % (Energy)	Fibre content %	Manufacturers' feed recommendations
Allen and Page Herbal quiet mix	9	10	2.5	14	Oat-free mix, containing mint, garlic, cloves and other herbs.
Allen and Page Herbal hacking mix	10.5	12	2.5	12	A feed for active horses and ponies. Useful at times of stress. Contains mint, garlic and a blend of other herbs.
Baileys No 8 meadow sweet	10	10	2.5	16	A non-heating, high fibre coarse mix for horses and ponies in light work. Contains spearmint, clover and comfrey.
Badminton Park mix	9.5	11	3	12	An oat-free, highly palatable, non-heating mix of cereals and pulses with the natural herbs, garlic, clover, rosemary and mint.

Table 3.16 Conditioning feeds

Feed	Energy MJDE/kg	Protein content CP%	Oil % (Energy)	Fibre content %	Manufacturers' feed recommendations
Allen and Page Show special mix	10.75	14	5	6	Formulated to produce weight and bloom on show horses and ponies.
Baileys No 1 cooked cereal meal	14	15	2.2	1.2	A complementary feed designed for use as part of a concentrate ration for improving condition and maintaining a topline on show horses.

Feed	Energy MJDE/kg	Protein content CP %	Oil % (Energy)	Fibre content %	Manufacturers' feed recommendations
Balanced Horse Feeds Show mix	10	10	3.5	19	A high fibre feed designed to promote extra condition required for the show ring. Ideal for show horses, stallions and resting competition horses that lose condition.
Spillers Conditioning cubes	13.4	15.5	4.25	8.5	Formulated for adult horses and ponies requiring optimum condition and topline.
Spillers Showing mix	13.3	13	4	8	Formulated for adult horses and ponies requiring optimum condition and topline.

Table 3.17 Veteran and convalescing feeds

Feed	Energy MJDE/kg	Protein content CP %	Oil % (Energy)	Fibre content %	Manufacturers' feed recommendations
Allen and Page Old Faithfuls special blend	11	10	3	8	A feed formulated to tempt the elderly or recuperating horse and pony. Contains probiotics and herbs.
Balanced Horse Feeds Invalid diet	9.8	12	3	11	A mix formulated for horses on box rest due to injury, age or disease.
Dodson and Horrell Sixteen plus	11.5	13	5.1	17	A feed formulated for the older horse and pony.
Dodson and Horrell Convalescent diet	No figure available	9.5	3.8	13.5	A mix designed for horses on box rest or in light exercise after suffering injuries.

Table 3.18 High fibre mixes and hay replacers

Feed	Energy MJDE/kg	Protein content CP %	Oil % (Energy)	Fibre content %	Manufacturers' feed recommendations
Allen and Page Fibre Pencils	8	10.5	2.5	22	An oat-free feed which provides a valuable source of dietary fibre.
Balanced Horse Feeds Alfalfa chaff	8	10.5	1	28	A chaff formed from a blend of alfalfa, oat straw and molasses.
Balanced Horse Feeds Show mix	10	10	3.5	19	A high fibre feed designed to promote extra condition required for the show ring.
Dengie Alfa-A	10	11.5	2.5	25	A lightly molassed chaff made of chopped dried alfalfa.
Dengie Hi-Fi	7	10.5	2	38	Hi-fi is designed to be fed in similar quantities to hay and may be used as a hay replacer or in combination with other forages.
Dodson and Horrell Fiber P	11.5	12	2.5	18	An alfalfa-based chaff with added cereals and herbs.
Main Ring Herbale	9.2	5	1	25	A short fibre forage equivalent to hay, with garlic, molasses, limestone flour and mint.
Spillers Total hay replacer	8.8	10.5	0.5	32.5	This feed offers an alternative to hay and may also be used as a chaff.
Spillers High fibre cubes	9.6	10	2.75	20	A low energy, high fibre maintenance diet for horses and ponies.
Spillers HDF cubes	12.5	13	4	19	Cubes formulated for competition horses, which deliver a good energy level from a high fibre diet.

Table 3.19 Feeds for medium work

Feed	Energy MJDE/kg	Protein content CP%	Oil % (Energy)	Fibre content %	Manufacturers' feed recommendations
Allen and Page Light competition mix	12.5	14	3.25	7	A mix suitable for the horse and pony in medium to hard work.
Badminton High energy coarse mix	11.25	11.5	3	8.5	A mix formulated for horses which require a higher level of energy, particularly youngstock.
Badminton Hunter event cubes	11	13	5.5	11	Cubes formulated for horses and ponies in hard work, training and competition.
Baileys No 4 topline cubes	13.5	12.5	2.7	4	Non-heating performance cubes formulated for horses and ponies in medium to hard work, or those needing to gain weight.
Balanced Horse Feeds Riding horse mix 1	12	12.5	4	9.6	A coarse mix designed for horses in medium work.
Dodson and Horrell Competition wafers	11.5	12	3.2	12.2	A feed formulated to provide the required nutrients for competition horses without causing over exuberance.
Dodson and Horrell Competition country mix	11.5	12	3.5	8	An ideal feed for competition horses.
Dodson and Horrell Development phase three	12.75	13	5.2	9	A high fibre, oat-free, non-heating performance feeding system for competition horses and ponies.
Main Ring Cool cubes	12.2	10	4.25	15	Cubes formulated without oats to meet the concentrate requirements of horses and ponies in light or moderate work
Spillers Competition cubes	11.3	12	3.75	14	A medium energy feed carefully formulated for eventers, showjumpers, carriage driving, endurance and team chasing.
Spillers Original mix	13.2	11	3	8.5	A mix designed for showjumpers, hunters, eventers, carriage driving, polo, endurance and team chasing.

Table 3.20 Feeds for hard and fast work

Feed	Energy MJDE/kg	Protein content CP %	Oil % (Energy)	Fibre content %	Manufacturers' feed recommendations
Allen and Page Competition extra mix	13.25	15	3.5	9.5	A high energy mix designed for eventers, hunters, polo ponies, chasers and Thoroughbreds in training.
Badminton High energy coarse mix	11.25	11.5	3	8.5	A mix formulated for horses which require a high level of energy, particularly youngstock.
Badminton Stockholm mix	11.9	11	3.5	6.25	A mix specially designed for the highly trained horse in peak condition.
Badminton Racehorse cubes	11.5	15	4.75	8	A cube formulated for racehorses in training and young competition horses in work.
Baileys No 4 topline cubes	13.5	12.5	2.7	4	Non-heating performance cubes formulated for horses and ponies in medium to hard work, or those needing to gain weight.
Baileys No 10 racehorse mix	14	13	8.5	8	A coarse mix designed as the sole concentrate ration for horses in hard work and at peak fitness.
Baileys No 11 racehorse cubes	14	13	8	5	A cube designed as the sole concentrate ration for horses in hard work and at peak fitness.
Balanced Horse Feeds High performance mix	13	13	4.5	9.3	A dust-free ration designed to meet the demands of horses in strenuous work.

Feed	Energy MJDE/kg	Protein content CP%	Oil % (Energy)	Fibre content %	Manufacturers' feed recommendations
Burgess Supa Horse	15.6	15.8	7	4	A non-heating boiled feed for horses in hard work, youngstock and breeding stock.
Dodson and Horrell Development phase three	12.75	13	5.2	9	A high fibre, oat-free, non-heating performance feeding system for competition horses and ponies.
Main Ring Gold High Performance mix	14.8	14	4	10.5	A quality coarse mix formulated to meet the requirements of horses showjumping, racing, eventing, endurance riding, hunting and polo.
Spillers High Performance mix	14	14.5	4	8	A coarse mix ideal for showjumpers, eventers, polo, harness racing, endurance riding and team chasing.
Spillers Racehorse cubes	13.2	11	4	8.5	A high energy diet formulated to meet the demands of the athletic horse.
Spillers Racing mix	14.3	14	4	7.5	A blend of cooked, flaked cereals selected to ensure maximum palatability and digestibility.

Table 3.21 Feeds for Stud stock

Feed	Energy MJDE/kg	Protein content CP %	Oil % (Energy)	Fibre content %	Manufacturers' feed recommendations
Allen and Page Foal pellets	13	17.5	4.5	9	A palatable, easily digested feed designed to supplement the mare's milk.
Allen and Page Stud pencils	12.5	17	3.5	7.5	A pellet specially formulated to meet the increased requirements of stallions and lactating or in-foal mares.
Badminton Breeder cubes	12	15.5	4.75	7	A high protein ration formulated to meet the demanding nutritional needs of the broodmare, stallion and growing foal.
Badminton Stud mix	12.5	15.5	4.5	7	A mix formulated for stallions, lactating mares and weanlings or yearlings that do not find cubes palatable.
Badminton Foal pellets	12	18.5	5.25	7	A high protein feed formulated for correct growth and development of the foal, weanling and yearling.
Baileys No 7 stud mix	12.5	16	4.7	7.5	A mix designed for broodmares during pregnancy and lactation, and for youngstock from three months to three years.
Baileys No 3 stud cubes	13.5	15	3	8.5	A compound feed formulated to meet the increased requirements of pregnancy and lactation.
Baileys Foal starter	13.5	18	8	4	A milk-based creep feed for foals up to three months of age and to supplement the diet when a mare is not feeding well.
Balanced Horse Feeds Developer foal starter	13	17.5	5	7	A coarse mix designed to supplement mares' milk and help prevent deficiencies in the foal.

Feed	Energy MJDE/kg	Protein content CP %	Oil % (Energy)	Fibre content %	Manufacturers' feed recommendations
Balanced Horse Feeds Developer weaning mix	12.8	16	4	8	This ration is formulated for foals 3–4 weeks after weaning. It contains high levels of amino acids and other nutrients to help promote optimum growth and development.
Balanced Horse Feeds Developer stud mix	12.5	15	4	9	This ration is formulated to meet the tremendous nutritional demands of broodmares in late pregnancy and lactation.
Dodson and Horrell Development phase one	12.1	15.5	3.1	6.5	A formulated feeding system for the growth and development of competition horses and ponies up to 12 months of age.
Dodson and Horrell Stud diet	12.8	15	3.7	6.2	A mix formulated for breeding mares.
Dodson and Horrell Breeding phase two	12.2	14.5	4.2	8.4	A feed formulated for competition horse and pony broodmares and youngstock from 12 months of age.
Spillers Breeding mix	13.6	16	4.25	7.5	A blend of cooked flaked cereals specially formulated to meet the nutritional needs of all breeding stock.
Spillers Stud cubes	13.6	16	4.25	7.5	A cube formulated to keep mares and foals in good condition. Maintains condition and fertility in working stallions.
Spillers Foal and yearling pellets	13.4	16.5	4.5	8.5	Pellets specially formulated to meet the needs of the growing foal.

Table 3.22 Balancing feeds to be fed with cereals

Feed	Energy MJDE/kg	Protein content CP%	Oil % (Energy)	Fibre content %	Manufacturers' feed recommendations
Baileys Oat balancer	15	16	12	5	A high energy pellet formulated to complement other grains.
Dodson and Horrell Oat balancer	12.5	17	5.6	8.5	A mix formulated to be fed with oats.
Spillers Oat balancer	13.4	20	4	7.5	A concentrate pellet specially designed to balance the nutritional deficiencies in oats and other cereals.

ROUGHAGE FEEDS

Roughages are the natural feed of the horse and should be the base of every diet. Horses have evolved over millions of years to be excellent roughage eaters. The wild horse survives purely off roughage feeds and they are very effective at gaining nutrients from what seems to be very poor grassland. The traditional roughage feed has always been grass and hay but over the years, with the ever increasing horse population and a run of very dry summers, horse owners have had to look for alternatives to hay.

The horse owner often neglects the roughage part of their horse's diet. We all tend to spend many hours deliberating over the choice of expensive concentrate feeds and then throw in flakes of hay without thinking about it. Consideration made to the roughage aspect of a diet will not only help the horse but will also help the financial outlay of the owner. Good quality hay contains the same energy value as a sack of horse and pony cubes but is half the price and contains the fibre needed to satisfy the appetite of the horse.

Fibre is essential to a horse as it:

- Maintains a healthy digestive system
- Satisfies the horse's appetite
- Provides an occupational therapy.

Meadow hay is full of a wide variety of grasses

There are two types of hay commonly fed to the horse, meadow hay and seed hay.

Meadow hay

Description
Is made from established permanent pasture land that contains a wide variety of grasses and possibly herbs. The fields are often grazed by livestock and then left for the summer to grow a hay crop. The quality of meadow hay varies widely according to the type of grass grown and the time of cutting. Some meadows contain an excellent variety of high quality grasses but others can contain poor quality grasses, resulting in poor quality hay. Good meadow hay should have a high proportion of leaf matter as this contains most of the nutrients from the grasses.

The grass species with the best nutritional value are:

- Timothy grass
- Meadow fescue
- Perennial rye grass
- Cocksfoot
- Fescues
- White clover.

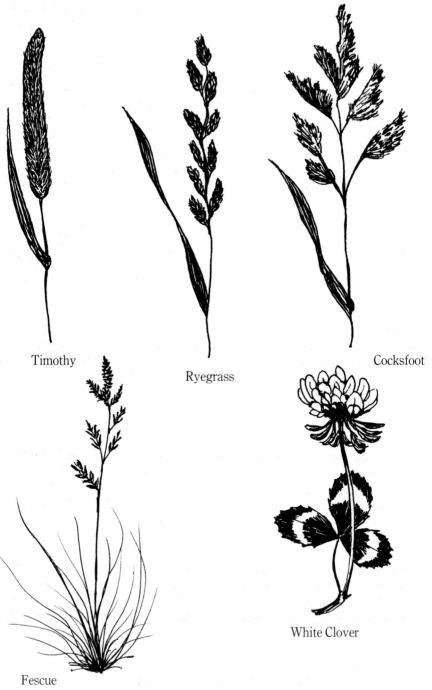

Timothy

Ryegrass

Cocksfoot

Fescue

White Clover

Figure 3.1 Good grasses

Permanent pasture land that contains more than 30 per cent perennial rye grass and a mixture of the illustrated grasses is classified as Class 1 grassland and produces the best hay.

The leaf is the most nutritious part of any grass and as the grass grows and becomes older the nutritional content drops and the whole plant becomes more stemmy with the indigestible lignin content increasing. Because the nutritional content of grass decreases with age the time that hay is cut has a direct effect on its nutritional value. The best time to cut for hay is as the grass just begins to flower and the seed head is starting to emerge from sheath. This hay will have the highest levels of protein (9–12 per cent). Unfortunately many hay producers leave the pasture land for as long as possible prior to cutting to gain the largest yields but by then the nutritional value has dropped and the fibre content has increased.

Advantages
Meadow hay is relatively soft and is palatable to most horses. If a good quality meadow hay is fed it will contain a variety of nutritious grasses and herbs that can provide the horse with a wide variety of nutrients. If you have a horse in light work or with laminitis you can select a meadow hay that contains the less energy-rich grasses.

Disadvantages
Nutritional content varies according to the grasses and date of cutting. It can contain weeds and toxic plants if not checked and managed correctly prior to cutting.

Seed hay

Description
The grasses used to make seed hay are specially selected and sown. The grasses chosen are usually rye grass based and may contain clover and timothy. This hay is treated as a crop and therefore tends to be more expensive. Seed hay is often coarser than meadow hay and usually takes longer to eat. The nutritional value of seed hay depends on the mix of grasses it contains.

Advantages
Seed hay can have a higher protein and energy levels than some meadow hays, which can be useful when feeding horses in medium or hard work. The hay is generally coarser in texture which requires more chewing and so takes longer to eat. Seed hay is unlikely to contain any weeds or toxic plants due to the sward being seeded.

Disadvantages
It is usually more expensive than meadow hay to buy.

Assessing the quality of hay

When buying hay it is essential that you can assess the quality of the bales. If you are cutting it yourself or have arranged to buy it off the field you have the opportunity to check the sward and monitor when it is cut and baled. Unfortunately most of us have to check the hay once it has been baled and this is not as easy as assessing the crop in the field.

There are a number of factors which will affect the quality of the hay and it can be useful to find out prior to purchase:

- If it is a first or second cutting. Some people take two cuttings from a field. The second cut is often preferable as it usually has a lower moisture content and fewer weeds.
- When the bales were cut. As mentioned previously an early cut is often preferable due to the higher protein levels.
- The age of the bales. Is the hay this year's crop or last year's crop.
- How the bales were dried. Field drying poses many more risks to the quality of hay than barn-dried hay. But barn-dried hay is more expensive.

Having gained as much information as possible on the background of the hay crop, you then need to get your hands dirty! It is important to check the hay in the middle of a number of bales from the stack as one bale could be exceptionally good or bad but will not give a true picture of the quality of the harvest. When checking a bale you should look for:

- Dust. The bale should be free from dust and if dust billows out as you remove some hay to check it, it is unlikely you will need to look any further! Research carried out recently stated that 90 per cent of the hay harvested in the UK was too dusty to be suitable for horses!
- Smell. The bale should smell sweet and fresh, not musty.
- Colour. The bale should be a green/yellowish colour, not brown or black.
- Grasses. You should be able to recognise the better grasses such as rye and timothy and look for them in the bale. There should also be a high percentage of leaf and flower heads present.
- Contaminants. Check the bales for any soil, weeds or poisonous plants such as ragwort.
- Moisture. The bale must be free from any moisture which will lead to moulds and possible heat build up resulting in the bales burning up.

When buying hay it can be a mistake to choose the cheapest bales. You may think you are saving money but cheap hay is likely to have a low nutritional value. This will mean that you have to use more concentrate feeds thus resulting in a higher concentrate feed bill! If you feed good quality hay it may be slightly more expensive but will save you money on concentrate feed and be healthier for your horse.

Hay storage

The way hay is stored can affect the nutritional quality of the bales. It should be stored in dry, well ventilated buildings and placed on pallets to allow air to circulate underneath. Hay stored incorrectly will become musty and mouldy as it cannot dry out correctly.

Properly harvested and stored hay bales should have a moisture reduction of 15 per cent if field dried and 35 per cent if barn dried. Unfortunately the British summer though good for grass growth is often not ideal for the drying of hay and much grass is baled too damp resulting in mouldy hay.

Any hay baled with a moisture content greater than 20 per cent undergoes extensive heating in the first 24 hours after baling. The extra moisture in the grass and the heat encourages the growth of fungus. These fungi increase the levels of acidity in the bale and this leads to the growth of many other moulds. These moulds feed on the natural sugars in the hay so reducing the nutritional content and more seriously they cause respiratory problems in horses fed mouldy hay.

Moulds and their effect on the horse

The feeding of mouldy, musty hay will have a dramatic and very damaging effect on the health and performance of your horse. Dealing with mouldy hay can also be very detrimental to the health of the horse owner. Breathing in spores can lead to Farmer's lung (hypersensitive pneumonitis) which is a debilitating disease.

Feeding mouldy hay has long been known as a health hazard associated with broken wind or chronic obstructive pulmonary disease (COPD). But there are other health risks which include botulism, bacterial infections and poisoning associated with mould contamination (mycotoxin poisoning).

There are a number of attempts to overcome the feeding of mould spores in hay as discussed below.

Soaking hay

This is the most common approach for reducing the spore content of hay but it is not always carried out correctly and can lead to other problems. The dry hay is submerged in a container full of water and left to soak for a period of time (ideally a maximum of half an hour). The hay is then drained and fed immediately. Soaking hay sticks the spore and dust to the hay so that the horse eats them rather than breaths them in.

When soaking hay certain factors need to be considered:

- Any soaked hay must be completely wetted as an area that remains dry can contain enough spores to damage the airways.
- On the other hand soaking hay for hours at a time can result in a leaching of the

nutrients. You are in fact washing out the spores and all the nutrient content of the hay so you are left with very clean roughage with very little feed value.

- The water the hay is soak in should be changed daily.
- Do not allow the hay to dry out after soaking as this will defeat the soaking process since the spores are once again released into the air and breathed in by the eating horse.
- Once a horse has become accustomed to eating soaked hay the airways can be even more sensitive to spores. This can mean that if dry, mouldy hay is fed the horse will suffer respiratory problems within an hour of being exposed to the spores. So once you have begun soaking hay ensure all hay fed is soaked, including hay used when travelling or at shows.

Steaming hay

Steaming is an alternative to soaking. The hay is placed in a container such as a plastic bin, boiling water is poured over this hay and the lid put on to keep in the steam. Boiling water is then added periodically to top up the steam. The hay is left for a period of time, drained and fed. Steaming tends to be less effective than soaking as it is harder to fully soak the hay. It is also more time-consuming and can only deal with small quantities of hay at a time.

Feeding barn-dried hay

Barn drying is meant to limit the moulding of the bales. The hay tends to be baled with a high moisture content and then dried out in ventilated barns using fans to increase air movement. This technique has helped reduce the spore count but there are still pockets of hay that miss the drying process and develop mould spores.

Feeding clean forage

The final alternative is to feed a forage that is only partially dried or wilted. This reduces the risk of the hay not drying out and generating mould spores. The common forages that undergo this process are horse silage and haylage.

Feeding silage to horses

Silage is the name given to a forage that has been sealed and allowed to 'pickle in its own juices'. Grass silage has been a traditional feed for cattle but in recent years it has become a roughage feed for horses. The silage is made from grass cut just after the seed heads appear. This grass is left to wilt for between 18–24 hours and then collected off the field either into bales, a clamp or silo. The wilted grass is sealed in airtight bags or a container and allowed to ferment. This fermentation of the sugars in the grass increases the acid levels in the grass and this prevents the growth of harmful bacteria, so preserving the grass.

It is essential that the grass ferments and reaches an acidic level of pH 4 in clamp silage and pH 5–6 in big bale silage in order to prevent the development of harmful bacteria. Should the acidity not be reached harmful bacteria can grow and produce butyric acids. This acid rots the silage (giving off a smell of ammonia) and forms toxic compounds which can poison the horse. Clostridial bacteria can also develop if the acidity is not reached and this can cause botulism in horses.

When introducing horses to silage it is essential to check for any contamination and to introduce it gradually into the diet to reduce the risk of digestive upsets.

Table 3.23 Nutritional value: silage

	Energy MJDE/kg	Crude protein %	Crude fibre %
Big bale silage	10	10	30
Clamp silage	9–10	11	30

Silage has a good calcium/phosphorous ratio.

Advantages of feeding silage
It is virtually free from dust, spores and fungus.
It is available even when hay is at a premium.
It usually has a higher nutritional value than hay.
It is easily digested due to the fermentation of the grasses prior to feeding.

Disadvantages
It can be contaminated and therefore poisonous to horses.
Cattle silage is often too rich for horses resulting in digestive disorders.
It is usually made in big bales or clamps which can be difficult to use.
Once the sealed bags have been opened it must be used quickly to prevent spoilage.

Haylage
Haylage is a mixture of hay and silage and is the most popular alternative to hay used today. Rye grass is cut before flowering, allowed to dry in the fields and then collected, compressed and sealed into airtight bags.

'Haylage'
Courtesy of Dengie Crops Ltd

While in the bags the grass undergoes a mild fermentation which changes the acidity of the grass and prevents fungal spores from growing. This makes it virtually dust-free.

Table 3.24 Nutritional value: haylage

	Energy MJDE/kg	Crude protein %	Crude fibre %
Haylage	9–12	9–12	30

Advantages of haylage
It is virtually free from dust, spores and fungus.
It is more nutritious than hay, which can be an advantage for horses that require a high level of nutrition.
It is accessible and when unopened has a good shelf life (18 months) so can be bought in bulk.
Is bagged in plastic so can be stored outside.
Horses find it palatable so it can be useful for fussy eaters or convalescing horses.

Disadvantages
It is richer than hay so you can easily overfeed it.
It is more expensive than hay.
It is very palatable so horses usually eat it quickly. This can lead to boredom or the horse gaining weight as you feed more to pacify the appetite.
Once the bags are opened they must be used within four days.
If a bag is ripped or damaged the air will spoil the haylage, so careful storage is essential.

Hydroponic grass
This is a form of grass grown in a specially designed cabinet and fed fresh to horses. The grass is grown from barley seeds placed in trays and put in the cabinet. The cabinet provides a warm, light, humid environment that encourages these seeds to germinate and within six days the grass is ready to be fed.

Advantages
The grass has a good nutritional value and is a fresh, succulent feed.
It is dust- and spore-free.
The grass is very similar to spring grass, so can be a useful feed for persuading mares to come into season early in the year.
It is palatable and can be a useful addition to the stabled horse's diet.

Disadvantages
You need to buy the equipment which can be expensive.
It is a labour-intensive system.
The machine can break down!

Straw
Barley and oat straw can be fed as an effective form of roughage, especially to ponies who are prone to laminitis or weight gain. Good quality straw is often less dusty than poor hay and though less nutritious it does provide a cheap filler when mixed with haylage or good quality hay.

Advantages
A good alternative to hay for ponies who tend to put on weight.
Can be fed ad lib to horses or ponies as a way of keeping their stomachs satisfied but not overdoing the energy levels.
Can be useful as an extender when mixed into the daily ration of hay or haylage.

Disadvantages
Has a low feed value which needs to be balanced with concentrates.
Can encourage horses to eat their straw bedding.

Legumes
Legumes are plants which can fix nitrogen from the soil, and as protein is made from nitrogen they have a high protein level. Common legumes fed to horses are clover, sainfoin and lucerne (alfalfa). Legumes are fed as hay or in cubes or chaffs.

Advantages
Legume hay has a higher nutritional value than hay.
There are a wide variety of high fibre, legume-based chaffs that can be used to improve the nutrient content of roughages such as straw or poor hay.
Alfalfa has good levels of protein and calcium so is a useful feed for young-stock.

Disadvantages
It is difficult to harvest in the UK so tends to be imported, which increases the price.

Table 3.25 Roughage feeds

Feed	Energy MJDE/kg	Protein content CP%	Oil % (energy)	Fibre content %	Comments
Poor meadow hay	6–7	3.5–6	1.7	33	The physical appearance and smell give a vague indication of the quality of the hay. A nutritional analysis is the most effective way of gaining a nutritional value of the hay.
Average meadow hay	7–8	5–8	2.6	31	Ditto
Good meadow hay	8–10	9–10	2.8	31	Ditto
Silage	12	15	4	30	Silage can be a good alternative to hay for competition horses or breeding stock that require higher protein levels.
Alfalfa hay	11	18	2.6	20.8	Alfalfa is legume hay that is rich in protein, calcium and vitamin A. It is excellent for competition horses and stud stock.
Italian rye grass – midbloom	2.5	4	0.9	4.7	These grass readings give an idea of the energy value gained by horses grazing but do not take into consideration the dilution of the energy when grazing other poorer grasses.

Feed	Energy MJDE/kg	Protein content CP %	Oil % (energy)	Fibre content %	Comments
Timothy grass – midbloom	2.5	2.7	0.9	9.8	See Italian rye grass.
Meadow fescue – midbloom	3	4.7	1.7	7.7	Ditto
White clover	2	5	0.9	2.7	Clovers are a rich source of protein in the grazing horse but can cause problems to laminitic ponies.
Red clover – full bloom	3	4.1	1	4.6	Ditto
Oat hay	7.5	8.6	2.2	29.1	Oat hay is cut at an early stage with the seed head intact.
Barley hay	8	7.8	1.9	23.6	Barley hay is cut at an early stage with the seed head intact.
Wheat hay	6.5	7.7	2	25.7	Wheat hay is cut at an early stage with the seed head intact.
Oat straw	5	3	0.8	40	Clean oat straw can make a useful alternative to hay when fed with a concentrate feed.

Hay cubes

Alfalfa is the most common legume used for cubed hay. Unlike alfalfa chaff or complete cubes, which are a mix of roughage and concentrate materials, the hay cube is made directly from alfalfa hay. The cubes are usually large (4 cm wide and 5 cm long). This larger size increases chewing time so minimising the risk of the horse becoming bored and chewing wood. Research done into feeding hay cubes has found that horses fed cubes as opposed to loose hay required less concentrate feed and this is thought to be due to less wastage by the horses eating the cubes.

Advantages

Cubes take up less storage space and are easier to store than bales of hay.
Less is wasted so it is more efficient.
The cubes do not fluctuate in nutritional value or availability like bales of hay.
It is a dust- and spore-free roughage feed.

Disadvantages

Some horses have experienced choke if they bolt the cubes when eating.
It is impossible to determine the quality of the forage used to make the cubes.
The cubes lack the long fibre required by the horse and this can result in the horse chewing wood.

CHOOSING THE RIGHT FEEDSTUFFS FOR YOUR HORSE

Name of your horse: . . . .

Date: . . . .

Section A

Age score:. . . . . .FROM ASSESSMENT SHEET 1

Condition score: . . . . .FROM ASSESSMENT SHEET 1

Temperament score: . . . . .FROM ASSESSMENT SHEET 1

Work done	Description	Score
None	Maintenance	5
Light	Hacking, light schooling and competing	4
Medium	Schooling and regular competing	3
Hard	3-day eventing, hunting and jumping	2
Fast	Racing, team chasing, point-to-pointing	1

Total score For Section A: . . . .

Section B

1. Nutrient demands: from assessment sheet 1

    Protein . . . .

Possible feed choices

Now you have read Chapters 3 and 4 select the feeds that you feel may suit your horse. This information can then be used when calculating a ration in Chapter 7.

1. For horses that score between 10 and 16 on Section A and have low protein demand of between 1 and 2 in Section B.

Straights	Compounds	Roughages
Oats	Cool mixes or cubes	Meadow hay
Sugarbeet	Quiet mixes or cubes	Dengie Hi-Fi
	High fibre mixes	
	Herbal mixes	

2. For horses that score between 8 and 10 in Section A and score between 2 and 3 in Section B.

Straights	Compounds	Roughages
Oats	Cool mixes or cubes	Meadow hay
Barley	Quiet mixes or cubes	Dengie Alfa-A
Sugarbeet	High fibre mixes	Alfalfa chaffs
	Herbal mixes	
	Show mixes	

3. For horses that scored between 6 and 8 in Section A and score 3 in Section B.

Straights	Compounds	Roughages
Oats	Light competition mixes	Meadow hay
Sugarbeet	Competition mixes and cubes	Seed hay
Peas and beans	Oat balancers	Alfalfa chaffs
Linseed		

4. For horses that scored between 3 and 6 in Section A and scored between 4 and 5 in Section B.

Straights	Compounds	Roughages
Naked oats	Competition mixes and cubes	Seed hay
Sugarbeet	Performance mixes	Lucerne hay
Soyabeans	Race mixes and cubes	Alfalfa chaffs
Peas and beans	Oat balancers	
Linseed		

CHAPTER 4
Feed Processing Techniques

Many feeds given to horses have been processed prior to feeding. We do this ourselves when we boil feeds, cut chaff and bruise whole oats. The feed companies take this processing one step further with complex cooking processes. Any processing of feeds is done to increase digestibility. The mechanical cutting and breaking down of grains opens up the tough outer coats which reduces the chewing time and allows all the digestive juices immediate access to the softer digestible kernels of the grain.

The cooking of grains changes the structure of the starch (gelatinisation) which makes it more easily digestible to the horse. This reduces the risk of digestive problems in the intestines as the cooked starch is broken down more rapidly and efficiently than raw starch.

A disadvantage of processing grains is that it can destroy the mineral and vitamin content and damage the protein and oil. This risk is minimised by cooking in the presence of water and often any mineral and vitamins destroyed in the process are replaced before bagging up the feed.

Processing is expensive and will often constitute at least 10 per cent of the value of the product, which is why compound feeds such as mixes are more expensive than straight grains such as oats.

COMMERCIAL PROCESSING TECHNIQUES

Steam flaking
This was the first method used to cook the starch in cereals and is commonly used on barley. Once the grain has been cleaned it is passed through a rotating damp wheel that adds water to it, as in order for the steam flaking to be successful the grain needs to have a moisture content of 20 per cent. The wet grain is dropped into oak wood damping bins and left to soak for 24 hours. In some cases chemicals are added to the grain to increase the absorption of the water during soaking.

After soaking the grain is passed into cookers that have steam injectors which cook the starch in the grain. Once steamed the feed passes directly on to rollers that flatten the grains and reduce the moisture content by about 2 per cent. Finally the rolled cereal is conveyed to dryers to reduce the moisture content further and once dried the grain is bagged or mixed into coarse mixes.

Micronisation

This is a method used to cook the starch in cereal grains. It is a common way of processing barley and maize. The grain is cleaned and sorted then spread onto a moving conveyor belt which carries it horizontally beneath burners which give out infra-red radiation waves. The waves rapidly heat the inside of the grains to between 150 and 180 degrees centigrade, making them swell and gelatinise. The cooked grains are then passed through rollers and cooled. The result is a cooked, flaked cereal which is more digestible, free from any moulds or bacteria and, in the case of soyabeans, no longer toxic to the horse.

Extrusion

This is another method of cooking the starch in cereal grains. The grains are cleaned, weighed and pre-conditioned, which involves injecting water and steam into the grain. The feed is then forced under high pressure through an extruder cooker. This cooker is very similar to a pressure cooker but with a continuous flow of steam passing through under high pressure and achieving very high temperatures.

Once the grain has been steamed for just long enough to soften and cook, the gluten part of the grain is passed through a die to form pellets. The sudden change in temperature from the cooker to the die causes the grain to puff up and develop the characteristic look of extruded feeds. Finally the pellets or nuggets are dried with hot air dryers at 300 degrees centigrade for twenty minutes, then cooled and bagged.

HOME COOKING PROCESSES

Due to the wide variety of processed feeds available less processing is done by the horse owner today but there are still some feeds that are cooked on the yard.

Boiled barley

Whole barley grains are boiled in water to cook the starch. Boiled barley is excellent for improving condition and weight and for feeding to tired or convalescing horses.

Method
Soak the whole barley in cold water for a minimum of 12 hours. Once soaked top up the water level so that it covers all the grain and bring the barley to the boil. Simmer for a number of hours until all the grains have swollen and split. Allow to cool to an edible temperature, drain and feed with chaff, linseed or the normal evening feed.

Linseed jelly

Linseeds are poisonous if fed raw so if you wish to feed linseed jelly or tea you must first cook the seeds. Linseed can be a valuable weekly addition to a horse's feed as it improves condition, is a rich source of protein and can help alleviate the discomfort of horses suffering from respiratory conditions. Any linseed cooked must be used within 24 hours.

Method

Weigh out the seed. Allow 0.5 kg per horse. Put in a large pan and cover with cold water. Soak the seeds for 24 hours. After soaking bring to the boil and simmer for 1–2 hours until all the seeds have split and the linseed is of a jelly-like consistency. Allow to cool to an edible temperature and mix with boiled barley or the evening feed.

Linseed tea is made in the same way as linseed jelly but more water is added to the seeds. Linseed tea can be used in a bran mash or as part of a gruel for ill horses.

Bran mash

This is a warm feed often given to tired or ill horses as it is easily digested. It can also be used as a laxative.

Method

Put 1.5 kg of wheat bran into a bucket. Pour a small amount of boiling water or hot linseed tea over the bran until it is damp. Stir thoroughly adding up to a tablespoon of salt and a large tablespoon of limestone flour. Cover the bucket with a clean tea towel or stable rubber and leave to cool. When cool enough feed to the horse.

CHAPTER 5
Feed Storage

The correct storage of feeds is essential if they are to maintain their nutritional value and stay free of moulds that could damage the health of your horse. Incorrect storage of feeds will cause the nutrient levels to fall and the feed will be less inviting to the horse and could lead to respiratory problems or digestive disorders such as colic.

STORING CONCENTRATE FEEDS

All concentrate feeds should be stored in a feedroom that is horse-proof and secure. The feedroom must be dry, well ventilated, cool in temperature and kept clean and hygienic. Any sacks of feed being stored should be stacked on pallets and kept out of direct sunlight and heat.

Correctly stacked concentrate feed

Open sacks of feed must be stored in vermin-proof containers. The ideal are galvanised feedbins as they cannot be chewed through. A cheap alternative is a plastic bin with lid, but these need to be checked for any holes or chewed areas.

Plastic rubbish bins are a useful alternative to a galvanised feed bin

Filling the bins

If you have a number of horses being given one type of feed you may need to empty the sacks into the feedbins to provide enough feed for a week or more. If this is the case it is essential that all the old feed is used and the bin is cleaned out before the new feed is poured in. If new feed is poured on top of old it will lead to moulds and the whole feed going musty.

If you do not have many horses or a number of feedbins available it can be easier and more hygienic to leave the feed in the sacks inside the bins. This system means there is no risk of contamination from old musty feed left in the bins. The sacks also contain all the nutritional information on the particular feed which can be useful to refer to on occasions.

READING THE FEED LABELS

All feed manufacturers are required by law to state certain nutritional facts on the sacks of compound feeds. This is a great help when devising a balanced diet and trying to find a feed that supplies your horse's specific requirements.

Many people do not read these labels and I have found that when buying compound feeds it is surprising how many sacks are for sale on the shelves that are either past their sell-by date or very close to it! If you bought a feed that was already days off the sell-by date the nutrient levels will have changed by the time you finish the sack so it is well worth the effort of reading the label to check the sell-by date before purchase. You would not buy any other food that is passed its best and the same rules should apply to horse feeds.

The feed labels are often stitched onto the base or top of the sack and can easily be missed if you are not looking for them. The label must contain information on:

The percentage by weight of crude protein (CP %) = protein contained in feed.
The percentage by weight of crude fibre = complex carbohydrates in feed.
The percentage by weight of crude oil = oil and fat contained in feed.
The percentage by weight of total ash = mineral matter in feed.

The amount of added synthetic vitamins A, D and E in international units (iu per kg).

If any antioxidant has been included to improve shelf life.

The most important information, which unfortunately does not have to be stated by law, is the energy content of the feed. Most manufacturers do now state this on the label and it is found in megajoules of digestible energy per kilogram (MJDE/kg). The feed sacks or labels also have information on the shelf life of the feed, the weight of the feed and any particular feed or storage instructions.

FEED CONTAMINANTS

Sunlight

Direct sunlight causes the destruction of a number of nutrients especially the B vitamin riboflavin. The heating effect that sunlight can have on sacks and bins will also have an adverse effect on the feed. Condensation is one of the most common causes of deterioration in feed. Moisture builds up on the inside of the feedbins and on the inside of sacks and this leads to mould developing and contaminating the feeds. Sunlight can also have a damaging effect on supplements stored in the feedroom and again will reduce their nutritional value.

Air

Fat soluble vitamins A, D, E and K and fatty acids found in feeds are subject to damage when they come into contact with oxygen (oxidation). Compound feed manufacturers add chemical substances that increase the life of these vitamins and fatty acids but they do not last forever. Any feed that is open to the air will suffer oxidation after a period of time but the time span must be stated by the manufacturer. The sell-by date on the sack will give you the shelf life of the vitamins and should be checked when you buy the feed.

Insects

Grain weevils, mites and beetles can contaminate feed. They accelerate the deterioration of the feedstuff, generate heat and moisture which leads to the production of fungus and mould spores. Beetles and weevils can be seen in grain and mites can be detected as they cause the feed particles to move! Contaminated feed will develop a sour smell and the horses will stop eating it. Insects thrive in dirty, damp, badly-stored grains and once they arrive they can be very difficult to get rid of. The best course of action is prevention and a clean, hygienic store with feeds kept at low temperatures in dry conditions is the best way to keep any insects at bay.

Vermin

Rats and mice are a common problem in feedrooms and, like insects, once they find a comfortable home they do not want to leave! Rats and mice will damage feed sacks and contaminate the feed with their urine and droppings. Not only does this affect the nutritional value of the feed, it can also affect the health of the horse and owner.

Mouse and rat droppings if inadvertently fed to horses can cause them to contract salmonellosis. Humans handling feed or equipment which has been contaminated by mice and rats can develop Weil's disease (leptospirosis). Maintaining a clean and hygienic feedstore will help prevent any infestation of rats or mice as will a yard cat or traps left in safe places in the feed store. Poisons should not be used unless laid by a qualified pest control person as the poison can get into the horse feed or poison other animals if not administered correctly.

STORING ROUGHAGES

The correct storage of roughages was discussed in Chapter 3 but in summary when storing hay or other roughage feeds the following points need to be considered:

- Hay should be stored in a dry, well ventilated building.
- The building should be downwind of the stables and horses to reduce the risk of

spores and dust affecting the horses. If the hay should catch fire it is also less likely to spread to the yard.

- The hay should be stacked safely on pallets to allow air to circulate under the stack.
- If you have a number of hay deliveries throughout the winter the older hay must be used first and so should be stacked at the front of the building and not mixed up with the new deliveries.
- Stored hay should be checked regularly for contamination from rats and mice and for any heating or mould occurring.
- Mouldy bales should be disposed of immediately so they do not contaminate the rest of the stack.
- Haylages or silages can be stored outside but care must be taken not to damage the sealed plastic bags. If a bag becomes pierced or ripped the haylage or silage must be used immediately or it will spoil.

CHAPTER 6

The Digestive Process

'Nutrients' is the term used to describe any substances that provide nourishment to the horse. They are found in feedstuffs and must be broken down into their most basic form in order to be digested by the horse. The nutritional requirements of the horse were discussed in Chapter 2 but these nutrients must get from the food into the horse's body in order to provide the nourishment the body requires and this is where digestion plays its part.

THE DIGESTIVE SYSTEM OF THE HORSE

Digestion is the name given to the process by which feeds are broken down into their simplest form. This breakdown of the food allows the horse to gain access to the nutrients that are needed by the body. When food is eaten it enters the mouth in a complex form. In this form it is much too large to pass through the walls of the intestines and be absorbed into the bloodstream. Therefore, if the horse is going to benefit from the nutrients in this food, it must be broken down into the smallest components possible and this is what occurs when food is digested, as shown below:

- Proteins are broken down into amino acids.
- Soluble carbohydrates are broken down into glucose.
- Fats and oils are broken down into fatty acids and glycerol.
- Complex carbohydrates are broken down into volatile fatty acids.

These broken-down nutrients can now be absorbed into the bloodstream and used for work, growth and repair or stored in the body.

The digestive system is, in simple terms, a very long tube through which the food passes. As the food travels along this tube it is mixed with a number of chemicals and bacteria which break it down. Near the end of the tube the nutrients released from the broken down foodstuff are absorbed and finally the waste products that are left are passed out of the body in the faeces.

It takes approximately 65–75 hours for food to pass through the digestive system when a horse is fed a traditional diet of cereals and roughage. So feeding an extra large or rich feed the morning of a competition is not going to give your horse any extra 'spring in his step'!

This system is designed to deal with a wide variety of feeds but some feeds are digested more efficiently than others. A working knowledge of the system allows the horse owner to feed a healthy diet that will provide all the necessary nutrients and be digested effectively and so reducing the risk of digestive disorders and vets' bills!

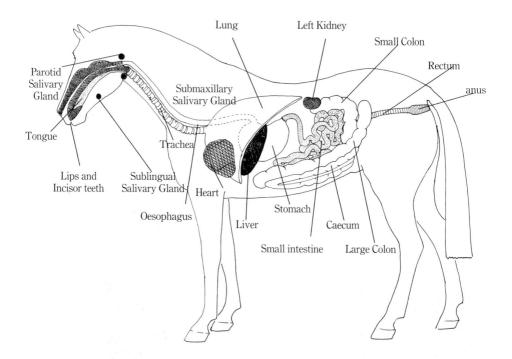

Figure 6.1 Diagram of the digestive tract, including salivary glands

The digestive system, also referred to as the alimentary canal, can be divided into eight parts:

1. The mouth and lips
2. The pharynx
3. The oesophagus
4. The stomach
5. The small intestine
6. The large intestine
7. The rectum
8. The anus.

The first three parts are involved in mechanical digestion, the physical breakdown of the food and the other five parts are involved in the chemical breakdown and absorption of the food.

THE MOUTH

This is the first stage of the digestive process.

The lips

The horse has very strong mobile lips covered with long, sensitive whiskers. These lips are used to choose the food and place it between the front teeth. Some horses are masters at this selection of feed and manage to eat a scoop of coarse mix but leave one ingredient that they dislike in the bottom of the bucket, which shows just how effective the lips are. It has also been known for horses that have had their whiskers trimmed to go off their feed, which is understandable when you are aware of how important they are in feed selection. When the horse is happy with the food it passes it through the lips and into the sharp incisor teeth where the food is bitten off.

A horse uses his lips to select the feed

The teeth

The main reason for a horse's head being so large is to house the roots of the large molar teeth that are needed to grind up the food. These teeth grow up from the gum and jaw continuously to replace the tooth that is ground away when the horse chews the feed. When eating, the food is bitten off by the incisors and ground and crushed very thoroughly by repeated 'side-to-side' sweeps of the molars at the back of the mouth.

Concentrate feed needs less chewing than hay as it is softer: 1 kg of hay will require 3,000–3,500 chews whereas 1 kg of concentrate needs only 800–1,200 chews before swallowing. This grinding action is made more effective through the conformation of the jaw. The upper jaw is wider than the lower jaw making the molar teeth overlap. This increases the effectiveness of the grinding action but does lead to sharp edges developing on the molars that can lead to mouth problems if the teeth are not rasped annually by a horse dentist.

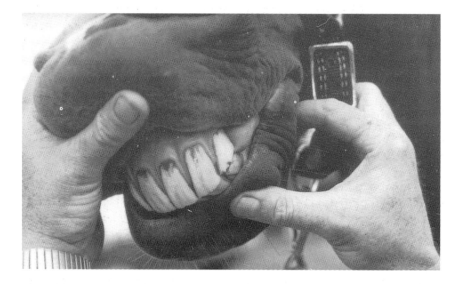

The horse's teeth should be checked regularly

Structure of the tooth

The construction of the tooth is essential for the efficient grinding of food. The tooth is comprised of three materials which differ in hardness: cement, dentine and enamel. The enamel is the hardest substance so is worn down the least. This results in the formation of hard enamel ridges which make a very effective grinding surface.

Chewing

The horse is the only herbivore that chews the roughage before swallowing and this chewing is an essential part of the digestive process. Chewing stimulates saliva production, which mixes the food into a paste.

A horse will chew different feeds for different lengths of time. Research has found that horses and ponies spend longer chewing short lengths of fibre than they do long lengths. Shorter lengths of fibre also take longer to eat than the longer fibre lengths. On average a horse will make 3,000–6,000 chewing movements on 1 kg of hay and 800–1,200 chews on 1 kg of concentrates.

Through chewing the food is broken down into very small pieces by the teeth and this has a dual effect:

1. The smaller pieces of feed have a much larger surface area than the large lump of feed so there is much more surface for the chemicals to act upon to further the digestive process.
2. The smaller pieces of feed will pass more easily along the tubes of the digestive system so are less likely to become stuck and cause obstructions.

If a horse is bolting his feed the food is not sufficiently chewed and therefore misses this vital first step of the digestive process. This has a knock-on effect as the digestive system acts rather like a production line: if the food is not dealt with correctly at the start of the production line the rest of the system will suffer. This results in the horse not receiving all the nutrients from the feed and possibly suffering from colic and other digestive disorders.

Teeth problems

Because the upper jaw in the horse is wider than the bottom jaw and the horse grinds in a continual side-to-side motion the molars can become worn, which leads to very sharp edges developing. If not checked these sharp edges can cut the cheeks and tongue, causing the horse pain when eating, so putting him off his feed. To prevent any mouth problems occurring horses should have their teeth checked by an expert at least once a year, ideally in the spring, after a winter of chewing hay.

Saliva

While the food is being chewed it is also being mixed with vast amounts of saliva produced by three pairs of salivary glands located in the jaw: parotid gland, submaxillary gland and sublingual gland. These glands produce about 10–12 litres (3 gallons) of alkaline saliva a day, which adds moisture to the food and helps to stick it together so forming a 'porridge' that can easily slide down the oesophagus.

The tongue

The tongue of a horse is composed of four parts:

1. A thick mucous membrane.
2. Muscles that contain nerves and blood vessels.
3. Salivary glands.
4. Taste buds.

The main role of the tongue is to move the food around the mouth, which breaks it down and mixes it with the saliva. The taste buds on the tongue provide the horse with information about the food before it is swallowed. This information is essential as once swallowed the horse cannot regurgitate the food so any problems must be detected before it passes down the oesophagus. It is thought that the horse can detect the taste of salty, sweet, bitter and sour elements in the feeds eaten. When the food has been thoroughly analysed by the taste buds and mixed with saliva the tongue pushes it to the back of the mouth and into the pharynx.

THE PHARYNX

The pharynx is a muscular passage that connects the mouth with the entrance to the oesophagus. This area of the throat is where air and food pass down two different tubes into the lungs and stomach. The trachea takes air into the lungs; the oesophagus takes food into the stomach. These two tubes lie next to each other and it is essential that the correct material passes into the correct tube, if food passes into the trachea and lungs the horse may die so there are two safety mechanisms to reduce the risk of such an accident occurring.

The first system involves two structures: The epiglottis and the soft palate. These structures provide a movable passage for the air or food to pass down the correct tube. When eating and swallowing the soft palate becomes raised so opening the entrance to the oesophagus. At the same time the epiglottis is folded back to form a lid over the trachea to prevent food passing down the incorrect tube. When breathing the soft palate lowers and the epiglottis moves into a forward position opening up the trachea for the passage of air.

The second safety mechanism is the coughing reflex. Should any food move into the entrance to the trachea the horse will respond with a violent coughing reflex which should propel the stray food back into the throat and away from the trachea to prevent it passing into the lungs.

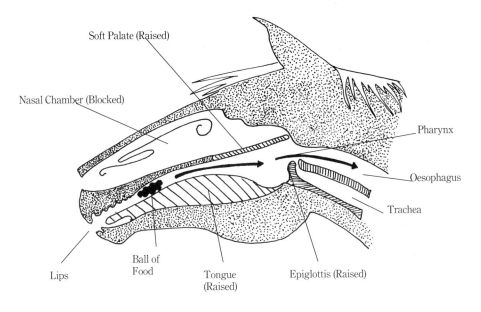

Figure 6.2 The process of swallowing

THE OESOPHAGUS

Once the food has successfully negotiated the pharynx it passes into the oesophagus. This is a tube of approximately 1.5 m in length (4–5 feet) which lies above the trachea along the left-hand side of the neck. No digestion occurs here, it is simply a passageway for the food from the mouth into the stomach.

The end of the oesophagus, which passes into the stomach, has a very strong band of muscle called the cardiac sphincter, which acts as a one-way valve. This valve prevents any food or gases passing back up the oesophagus once swallowed. For this reason vomiting and burping are very rare and only occur in cases of extreme illness.

THE STOMACH

The stomach is a small, muscular, J-shaped sac in which chemical digestion by enzymes begins. The stomach can only hold 9–18 litres (2–4 gallons). This is due to the fact that horses are by nature trickle feeders, which means they eat very small amounts over long periods of time, so the stomach never needs to hold more than 18 litres of food and saliva. This fact should be carefully considered when feeding horses concentrate feeds. If you give a horse more than 3 kg of feed per feed, once this has been mixed with saliva it will overfill the stomach which can lead to:

111

1.	The food not being correctly digested and the horse not receiving all the nutrients from this food.
2.	Food being forced into the small intestine before it has been broken down by the gastric juices.
3.	A risk of colic and other digestive disturbances occurring.

Therefore there are definite advantages to splitting the concentrate into a number of small feeds given throughout the day.

The stomach can be divided into four regions:

The Oesophageal Region
This is the storage area for food coming into the stomach from the oesophagus. No digestion occurs here.

The Cardiac Region
This area contains glands which secrete mucus.

REGIONS OF THE STOMACH

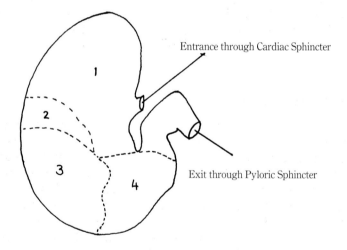

Entrance through Cardiac Sphincter

Exit through Pyloric Sphincter

Figure 6.3 Diagram of regions of the stomach

1. Non-Glandular Oesophageal Region
2. Cardiac Gland Region
3. Fundic-Gland Region
4. Pyloric-Gland Region

The Fundic Region
This area forms the main body of the stomach and contains all the gastric glands. These glands produce: hydrochloric acid to dissolve the mineral matter of the food; enzymes such as: PEPSIN to break down proteins and
                          LIPASE to break down fats.

The Pyloric Region
This is the part of the stomach which leads to the small intestine. It contains pyloric glands which produce more enzymes and mucus.

When a horse is able to eat 'little and often' the stomach is never empty. This is important as the hydrochloric acid is constantly pouring in and is not triggered by food. Should the stomach be allowed to become empty the hydrochloric acid present can damage the stomach lining and cause the horse discomfort. It will also lead to problems occurring further down the system.

Food lies in layers in the stomach with the heavier roughages tending to settle at the bottom and the concentrates lying nearer the top. This layering allows the denser feeds to stay in the stomach for longer as they require more time to be broken down by the gastric juices.

Food does not usually stay in the stomach for long. It is dependent on the type of food eaten and ranges from 30 minutes to 3 hours. When the food has been sufficiently worked on by the gastric juices it leaves the stomach, passing through the pyloric sphincter into the small intestine.

THE SMALL INTESTINE

The small intestine is where most of the breakdown and absorption of the concentrate feeds occur. It is here that the oats or mix are fully broken down and passed into the bloodstream to provide the horse with energy. The roughage is not absorbed until it reaches the large intestine. The ingesta (food) is moved through the intestines by muscular contractions known as peristalsis.

This section of the digestive system has a capacity of 70 litres (16 gallons), is approximately 26 metres long (80 feet) and when empty it has a maximum diameter of about 5 centimetres (2 inches). There is very little space available inside the horse to fit 26 metres of tubing so it has to be very tightly packed with many coils, loops and folds. These tight folds and the narrowness of the tube increase the likelihood of food becoming jammed or stuck, which results in colic. The likelihood of food becoming stuck in the small intestine is further increased when the horse is overfed and food is pushed through into the intestine having not been fully digested in the stomach.

The small intestine is suspended and supported by a strong sheet of muscular tissue known as the mesentery. The mesentery holds the folds in place but allows the intestines to move freely and for the food to pass along unhindered.

The small intestine is composed of three parts:

- The duodenum
- The jejunum
- The ileum.

The duodenum

This section is attached to the stomach and is approximately 1 metre in length forming an S-shaped curve around the pancreas. Ducts open into the duodenum from the pancreas and liver and release a constant flow of pancreatic juices and bile which combine to break down and extract the remaining fats, soluble carbohydrates and proteins from the concentrate feeds.

The small intestine adds approximately 100 litres (20 gallons) of digestive juices to the food each day. Pancreatic juices contain the enzymes:

Trypsin   breaks down proteins into amino acids.
Amylase   breaks down starch into maltose.
Maltase   breaks down maltose into glucose (simple sugar).

The duodenal (Brunner's) glands are found in this section of the intestines and produce enzymes to assist in the breakdown of the food. These enzymes include: sucrase, maltase and lactase which break down carbohydrates into simple sugars; and erepsin which breaks down proteins into peptides.

The jejunum

The jejunum is the longest part being about 20 metres (60 feet) in length. It contains intestinal glands and Peyer's patches, which produce enzymes to break down the food.

The ileum

This is the final section of the intestine and is about 1.5 metres (4.5 feet) long. It also contains intestinal glands and Peyer's patches and connects with the caecum of the large intestine at the ileocaecal valve.

The whole of the small intestine is lined with thousands of small finger-like projections called villi. These villi increase the surface area of the intestines and are responsible for absorbing the nutrients released from the food. The nutrients pass through the walls of the villi and into the blood capillaries and lymph system to be transported to the tissues in the body.

The majority of the nutrients released from the concentrate feeds will be absorbed at this stage of the digestive process. The remaining food should consist of roughage which is moved through into the large intestine.

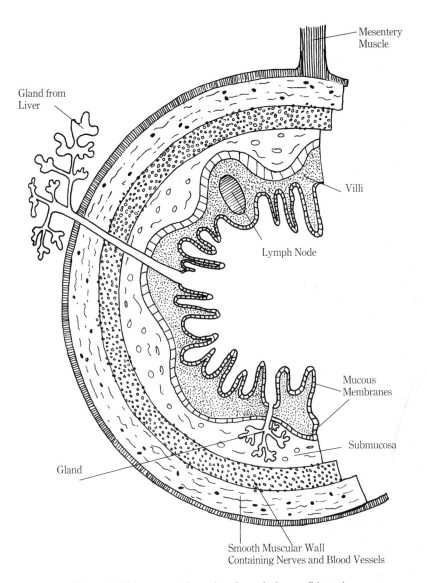

Mesentery
Muscle

Gland from
Liver

Villi

Lymph Node

Mucous
Membranes

Submucosa

Gland

Smooth Muscular Wall
Containing Nerves and Blood Vessels

Figure 6.4 Diagrammatic section through the small intestine
Adapted from Inside the Horse *Peter Rossdale (1976)*

THE LARGE INTESTINE

This section of the digestive system is responsible for breaking down and absorbing the nutrients from the roughage part of the food. Very little digestion occurs to the roughage until this point because roughage needs a very specialised form of digestion to extract the energy and that involves fermentation by bacteria. Digestion by fermentation generates a large amount of heat which can be very beneficial to horses or ponies wintering out but can be a problem with eventers or racehorses working in hot climates.

The large intestine is about 8 metres (25 feet) long and can be divided into four parts:

- The caecum
- The large colon
- The small colon
- The rectum and anus.

The caecum

The food passes into the caecum through the ileocaecal valve. The caecum is a sac, rather like the stomach but can hold 35 litres (8 gallons) of roughage and water. The caecum houses millions of bacteria known as gut flora or microbes.

There are forty-four species of bacteria which ferment the roughage to release energy in the form of volatile fatty acids (VFA). The number and type of bacteria in the large intestine are dependent on the type of ration being fed.

Gut flora are very sensitive to the type of food they ferment and if there is a sudden change in the food given to the horse it can cause millions of these bacteria to die off. This results in poor digestion of the roughage due to a change in the proportions of live bacteria. The dead bacteria can give off toxins (poisons) which pass into the bloodstream and cause blood poisoning and problems such as laminitis. It is, therefore, essential that these bacteria are given time to adapt to any new feed, hence the rule 'change feeds gradually'.

The bacteria are very useful to the horse. Not only do they break down the roughage, they also make vitamin B and vitamin C. It is important to consider the gut bacteria when your horse is on a course of antibiotics. Not only will antibiotics kill off the bad bacteria they will also kill off the good 'gut bacteria', which can lead to digestive disorders.

The large colon

As its name suggests the large colon has a large capacity of 110 litres (24 gallons) and a length of 4 metres (12 feet). Like the small intestine it is folded up to fit into the available space. The large colon has four distinct folds and each of these are areas where obstructions and blockages of food often occur, causing colic.

The large colon is responsible for further bacterial fermentation and absorption of nutrients and is the main area for water absorption from the feedstuffs. When horses are fed high proportions of roughage or grass with a high cellulose content the ingesta is bulky and when mixed with water becomes very heavy (imagine the weight of 10 kg of soaked hay!). This bulk fills out the large colon and produces what is often called a 'grass belly'.

A high roughage diet is natural to the horse, and the weight of the ingesta is essential in order to keep the large colon in place, as, like the small intestine, it is suspended from the muscular mesentery. If the horse has a restricted roughage diet this provides a 'streamline' figure but can lead to problems when the large colon becomes too light and can twist and turn, leading to colic and twisted gut.

The roughage ingesta usually remains in the large intestine for between 36 and 48 hours before passing onto the small colon.

The small colon

The small colon is about 4 metres (12 feet) in length with a capacity of 16 litres (3.5 gallons). By the time the food reaches this part of the digestive system all of the work should have been done. There is a small amount of water absorption from the ingesta but the contents of the small colon are mainly solid waste material made from indigestible food matter. The small colon contains sac-like structures that form the material into loose balls which characterise horse droppings.

The rectum and anus

No digestion or absorption occurs here, it is simply a storage area. The rectum is a short, straight tube that holds the waste material until it is ready to be passed out of the anus.

NUTRIENT TRANSPORTATION

Once the nutrients have been broken down by the digestive process they are passed through the permeable walls of the small or large intestine and into the blood or lymph system. The bloodstream transports the amino acids, vitamins, minerals and soluble carbohydrates (now in the form of glucose) to various parts of the body. The lymphatic system transports the fatty acids and glycerol around the body.

THE USE AND STORAGE OF NUTRIENTS

The digested nutrients can be dealt with by the body in a number of ways:

- Glucose in the blood can be used immediately by the muscles as a rich energy source.

117

- Proteins now in the form of amino acids are used by all the cells of the body for growth, repair and renewal. There could also be an immediate demand for milk production in lactating mares.
- Fatty acids can be passed into the blood and these blood fats are another immediate source of energy to the horse.
- Water-soluble vitamins need to be used immediately by the cells in the body as they are not stored. Although this is not normally a problem as the horse produces his own vitamin B complex and C in the hind gut.
- Fat-soluble vitamins are used by the cells for a wide variety of functions discussed earlier and are transported around the body in the blood.

STORAGE

Soluble carbohydrates
Glucose from soluble carbohydrates if not required immediately can be stored. Storage takes place in a number of locations in the body: the liver stores glucose as liver glycogen; and the muscles store glucose as muscle glycogen.

Proteins
Protein in the diet if not required immediately can be stored. The spare amino acids are broken down in the liver to release energy which is stored as fat.

Fats
Fatty acids are stored very effectively as storage fat in the body in various locations: around delicate organs, for example, the liver; and in subcutaneous fat under the skin.

Fat-soluble vitamins
These vitamins can be stored in the storage fat and are usually stored around the liver.

Minerals
Minerals can be stored if not required immediately and can actually build to dangerous levels if continuously overfed in the diet. Certain trace minerals such as copper (Cu), selenium (Se) and molybdenum (Mo) can eventually produce toxic symptoms if overfed, which will lead to the slow poisoning of your horse!

CHAPTER 7
Planning a Diet for Your Horse

Having gained an awareness of the nutritional requirements of the horse and how these nutrients are digested and used by the body, you now need to ensure your horse is receiving all the correct nutrients in a balanced diet that fulfils all the horse's individual requirements. Feeding a correctly formulated diet is the only way to ensure that your horse is receiving the proper amount and balance of nutrients he requires.

You can guess a horse's diet and feed using your 'eye and judgement' but it can lead to deficiencies if not feeding a compound feed and as we all tend to lean towards the generous side when giving out the food it is likely that you could save money on your feed bill by formulating a diet and weighing your feeds.

Before you even start to decide what type of feeds to give your horse you need to consider a number of factors that will provide you with your individual horse's dietary requirements. These factors are discussed below.

GENERAL CONSIDERATIONS FOR PLANNING A DIET

As discussed in Chapter 1, the general factors that influence your horse's feed requirements are:

- State of health
- Condition
- Work done
- Age
- Temperament
- Breed
- Size
- Seasons
- If the horse is stabled or living out.

The worksheet at the end of Chapter 2 enables you to assess these general factors but you must also consider:

- The rules of feeding and ensure they are followed
- The nutritional requirements of your horse
- The energy and protein demands.

These are covered in detail in this chapter.

RULES OF FEEDING

When working out a feed regime you need to think about the 'rules of feeding' to ensure optimum conversion of all the available nutrients. The rules that require consideration when planning a diet are as follows.

Feed according to the work done

When formulating a feed the energy requirements of the horse must be met but not overfed. You need to objectively analyse how much work your horse actually *does*, not should do! Then feed enough energy to supply this demand. Overfeeding of energy leads to numerous problems such as over-exuberant horses, weight gain, laminitis and increased growth rate leading to problems like developmental orthopaedic disease. Underfeeding energy leads to poor performance, loss of condition and poor growth rates in youngstock.

Feed good quality feeds only

Horses must never be fed poor quality feeds as they can cause a variety of problems: dusty feeds will cause respiratory problems; poor quality feeds may be cheaper to purchase but are likely to have a low nutritional value meaning that you have to feed more to provide the required level of nutrients making it a false economy; mouldy feeds cause digestive disorders like colic as a horse cannot be sick.

Feed according to the bodyweight

This is a much more accurate way of feeding your horse and will reduce the risk of over or underfeeding. Often horses that are the same height can have a 50 or 60 kg difference in weight which should be accounted for in the diet. As a general rule the larger the horse the more feed it will require.

Each concentrate feed should be no larger than 2 kg (4 lb) in weight

The horse has a very small stomach due to being a 'trickle-feeder', eating little and often. If you feed more than 1.5 kg (3 lb) of concentrates there is a risk of over-filling the stomach and a dramatic increase in the amount of soluble carbohydrates escaping digestion and absorption in the small intestine. This results in the horse not obtaining all the nutrients he should. It can also lead to digestive upsets such as excess gas production, colic, laminitis and blockages as undigested feed is forced from the overfull stomach into the small intestine.

Feed at the same time every day

Horses are creatures of habit and seem to have an excellent built-in alarm clock set for feeding times! Research done into feed habits of the horse report that horses fed at irregular times exhibited many signs of stress and had a much higher tendency to chew wood than horses fed at the same time every day. Irregular feeding can cause changes in the movement of food through the intestines and bloodflow which increases the risk of colic.

Feed plenty of roughage

Roughage is the natural feed for horses. They have evolved over millions of years to live off a high roughage diet and the digestive system is very efficient at gaining nutrients from grasses and other high fibre feeds. Horses on limited roughage diets tend to suffer increased bouts of colic and digestive disturbances. To reduce the risk of colic the roughage part of the diet should not fall below 50 per cent of the total feed provided.

Change feeds gradually

You should spend between 7 and 10 days changing a horse onto a new feed, gradually introducing the new feed at a rate of no more than 0.2 kg (0.5 lb) each day. This allows the microflora in the large intestine to adjust to the new feed and will prevent digestive problems like diarrhoea and colic. This rule should also be followed when turning a horse out to grass, especially when they have been stabled or move to spring grass. Moving from one pasture to another is a change in diet and is often the reason for horses droppings becoming loose.

When horses are being turned out onto lush pasture it can help to give them their normal ration of hay before turning out and only turn out for short periods initially. This will give the digestive system time to become accustomed to the new grass and will reduce the occurrence of diarrhoea and colic.

Always weigh feeds

It may seem a performance at first but weighing feeds is the most efficient and correct way to feed a horse. Once you know how much a scoop of your feed weighs you may not have to weigh the feed every day but it is essential to work in weights not scoops.

If you work in scoops and change feeds from nuts to mix you will alter your horse's diet from one scoop of pony nuts weighing 1.35 kg (3 lb) to one scoop of mix which weighs 0.65 kg (1 lb), so reducing your horse's daily feed by 0.70 kg a day. Quite a substantial reduction!

Your scoops can also alter in size depending on who feeds and how generous you feel that day whereas the weight of a feed never fluctuates if measured correctly. Weighing feeds makes it very easy to calculate your feed requirements for a week or month when ordering feed and saves money as you never feed any more than is required.

NUTRITIONAL REQUIREMENTS

As discussed in an earlier chapter each horse has specific nutritional requirements that need to be fulfilled in any diet plan. In most good quality feeds the mineral and vitamin requirements are fulfilled but careful consideration must be made to the energy and protein provision.

FORMULATING A RATION

How much to feed?

The first figure to ascertain is the appetite of your horse and this is based on the bodyweight. There are a number of ways to find out how much your horse weighs, some methods being more accurate than others.

Weighbridge

This is the most accurate method but the least accessible to most horse owners. Some vet clinics have a weighbridge they may let you use and some feed companies have a portable weighbridge that they take to lecture demonstrations. If you are able to get to a weighbridge it is worth the effort as it gives you an exact figure to work from.

Weightape

This is a much more accessible method to use but is not as accurate. Accuracy varies but it does give you a figure to work from and if you own a tape it means you can keep a regular check on the change in weight of your horse. For Thoroughbred-type horses the weightape is relatively accurate but as the horse becomes heavier in build the tape becomes less accurate and can be out by 20 per cent.

Calculations

There are calculations devised by Milner and Hewitt in 1969 that are based on the girth and length of your horse from point of shoulder to point of buttock, which give you an approximate bodyweight. They are the same calculations that are used to design the weightape, but on the tape the hard work has already been done for you!

For bodyweight in kg: $$\frac{\text{girth (cm)2} \times \text{body length cm}}{8717}$$

For example: 16 hh horse $= \dfrac{160 \text{ cm} \times 176 \text{ cm}}{8717} = 517 \text{ kg bodyweight}$

For bodyweight in lb: $\dfrac{\text{girth (in)}2 \times \text{body length inches}}{241}$

For example: 16 hh horse $\quad = \quad \dfrac{60 \text{ inches} \times 76 \text{ inches}}{241} = 1135 \text{ lb body weight}$

Table of weights

This is the easiest method as you just need to know the height of your horse but it is the least accurate. Tables are produced in many books (like this one!) that give you the height and weight of a variety of horses. The problem is they do not take into account the condition and build of your particular horse, as one 15 hh horse can weight 20 kg more than another.

Table 7.1 Table of weights

Height	Type	Light build kg	Medium build kg	Heavy build kg
10 hh	pony	150	180	200
11 hh	pony	200	220	270
12 hh	pony	280	300	320
13 hh	pony	300	320	340
13 hh	foal/weanling	200	220	240
14 hh	pony	350	370	390
14 hh	weanling	350	370	400
14.2 hh	pony	400	430	460
14.2 hh	cob	450	500	530
15 hh	hack	400	450	500
15.2 hh	small hunter	475	500	520
16 hh	Thoroughbred	525	550	575
16 hh	hunter	575	610	630
16.2 hh	hunter	600	650	700
17 hh	draught	760	810	860

Appetite

Once you have ascertained the bodyweight of your horse, you can calculate the appetite. The appetite is the *maximum* that a horse should be fed each day. This includes all the grass, hay and concentrates. There is no reason why you should not reduce this figure or work to a lesser figure if your horse is a good doer, in good condition or on the plump side!

The appetite is normally 2.5 per cent of a horse's bodyweight but some people use 2 per cent of bodyweight if calculating the appetite for a pony or plump horse. When calculating the bodyweight of lactating broodmares or foals you may wish to use 3 per cent as they have the highest nutritional demands.

Appetite $\quad = \quad \dfrac{\text{bodyweight} \times 2.5}{100} \quad = \text{horse's appetite in kg}$

For example: 16 hh horse $\quad \dfrac{517 \text{ kg} \times 2.5}{100} \quad = 13$ kg of food per day (dry weight)

This example shows that this 16 hh horse should eat a maximum of 13 kg a day of dry matter, that is the food without the water content. Any wet feeds such as wet hay or sugarbeet should, therefore, be weighed and considered when dry before the water is added.

ENERGY DEMANDS

The energy-providing nutrients make up 80–90 per cent of the food consumed by the horse. Once your horse's general requirements are worked out, you need to assess the horse's energy requirements. This relates to the energy that is being used by the horse's body. If it is being used up it needs to be replaced if the horse is to maintain health and condition, performance.

The energy requirements of a horse can be split into two areas:

- Energy for maintenance: this energy demand is based on a resting horse that does not increase or reduce in bodyweight and can keep all systems working effectively.
- Energy for performance: this is the extra energy that is required for a specific function such as work, growth, pregnancy or lactation.

Energy requirements for maintenance
This is the energy that the horse requires to maintain health and condition. It is the energy used for:

- running of all the systems
- repair and renewal of the systems
- heat production.

The energy requirements for maintenance tend only to be affected by the seasons, as cold weather will increase the heat production, and so increase energy demand. In a stabled horse the maintenance requirement will usually stay at a similar level throughout the year, whereas a grass-kept horse will have a more variable maintenance requirement depending on the weather conditions.

It is essential when formulating diets and assessing energy that you use your eye alongside the calculations as every horse's requirements will vary and these variations need to be noted and considered.

Calculating the energy required for maintenance
The following figures provide a guideline to work with to calculate the MJDE needed for maintenance.

Megajoules of Digestible Energy per day (MJDE/day) = 18 + $\frac{\text{bodyweight (kg)}}{10}$

Table 7.2 Approximate figures for maintenance requirements of three horses

300 kg bodyweight (13 hh)	450 kg bodyweight (15 hh)	600 kg bodyweight (16 hh)
48 MJDE per day	63 MJDE per day	78 MJDE per day

In most diets the majority of maintenance energy requirements are provided by the roughage ration of the diet.

Energy for performance
This is the extra top-up of energy needed to supply the demand of specific requirements. This chapter will discuss the energy needs in the working horse, the growing horse and breeding stock.

The working horse
The harder a horse works the more energy it will use. This results in a higher demand of energy from the feed. Certain factors can increase the energy requirements for work:

- The weight carried by the horse (tack and rider).
- The intensity of the work – intense work increases energy demand.
- The duration of the work – long workouts use more energy.
- The terrain – rough, uneven terrain will increase energy demand.
- The incline – hill work increases energy requirements.
- The horse's state of fitness – fit horses use the available energy more efficiently.
- The weight of the horse – a heavy horse will have a higher energy demand.
- The weather – cold, wet conditions can increase energy demand.
- The action of the horse – any deviations in action such as dishing can increase energy demands.

The energy requirements needed for the work done are calculated in relation to the bodyweight of the horse. The table below gives a work score that is used to calculate the **additional** megajoules required when the horse is in work.

125

Table 7.3 Work score for calculating performance energy demands

Type of work	Work score	Additional MJDE per 50 kg bodyweight	Extra energy needed by 400 kg horse (15 hh)	Extra energy needed by a 500 kg horse
1 hour walking	1	+1	50/400 = 8 x 1 = 8 MJDE	10 MJDE
1 hour walk and bursts of trot work	2	+2	50/400 = 8 x 2 = 16 MJDE	20 MJDE
1 hour work of walk, trot and canter	3	+3	50/400 = 8 x 3 = 24 MJDE	30 MJDE
Schooling: dressage or jumping	4	+4	50/400 = 8 x 4 = 32 MJDE	40 MJDE
Novice one-day event (ODE)/ hunting weekly	5	+5	50/400 = 8 x 5 = 40 MJDE	50 MJDE
Intermediate ODE/ Novice 3-day event/ hunting 3 days a fortnight	6	+6	50/400 = 8 x 6 = 48 MJDE	60 MJDE
Advanced ODE/ intermediate 3-day event/ hunting 2 days a week	7	+7	50/400 = 8 x 7 = 56 MJDE	70 MJDE
Racing	8	+8	50/400 = 8 x 8 = 64 MJDE	80 MJDE

Adapted from Horse Nutrition and Feeding *by Sarah Pilliner (1993).*

This table is used to estimate the additional energy the working horse will require above the maintenance requirements needed when in work. It is designed to be used as a guide as every horse is different and additions or reductions need to be made to the score when other factors that affect the horse's performance requirements have also been accounted for. Your eye will tell you if your calculations are correct. If the horse is putting on weight and getting a little full of himself then it is likely that your calculations are on the generous side and the energy requirement needs reducing. If on the other hand your horse is not performing as he should and is dropping some weight it could be that the energy requirement is too low and needs to be increased. Feel, common sense and science need to be used in conjunction to give the ideal diet plan, if you ignore one aspect you could find problems occurring.

Total energy requirements for the working horse
Having considered the maintenance and performance energy demands of your horse you then add the two figures together.

Maintenance energy + Performance energy = Total MJDE per day

Our 16 hh, 517 kg example horse is working for an hour a day in walk, trot and canter so falls into the +3 work score.

So the maintenance energy requirement is $\quad 18 + \dfrac{517\ kg}{10} = \quad$ 69.7 MJDE/day

Performance energy requirement is $\qquad \dfrac{517}{50} \times 3 = 31$ MJDE/day

Therefore the total energy requirement for this horse is $\qquad 69.7 + 31 = 100.7$
rounded up to 101 MJDE/day

FORAGE TO CONCENTRATE RATIO

The work level of the horse will determine what ratio of forage to concentrates the horse will require. The harder the work, the higher the concentrate part of the feed. In order to maintain a healthy digestive tract and minimise the risk of colic and other digestive disturbances, the forage part of the ration should be reduced to no less than 45 per cent and ideally go no lower than 50 per cent of the total feed. The table below gives some example ratios for the work done.

Table 7.4 Forage to concentrate ratios

Work score	Energy from forage %	Energy from concentrates %
Maintenance	100–90	0–10
1–2: light	90–70	10–30
3–5: medium	70–60	30–40
6–7: hard	50–40	50–60
8: fast	30	70

The total energy requirement of our example horse is 101 MJDE per day. The horse has a work score of 3 so from this 101 MJDE a ratio of 70 per cent forage and 30 per cent concentrates would be sufficient.

$$\text{Forage} = \frac{101 \text{ MJDE} \times 70}{100} = \quad 71 \text{ MJDE from forages}$$

$$\text{Appetite} = \frac{13 \text{ kg} \times 70}{100} = \quad \text{in maximum of 9 kg of feed}$$

$$\text{Concentrates} = \frac{101 \text{ MJDE} \times 30}{100} = \quad 30 \text{ MJDE from concentrates}$$

$$\text{Appetite} = \frac{13 \text{ kg} \times 30}{100} = \quad \text{in maximum of 4 kg feed}$$

At this stage we have all the figures we need, it is now just a case of deciding which feeds will best provide these energy demands.

PROTEIN REQUIREMENTS FOR THE WORKING HORSE

Before you move on to the selection of your horse's feeds you need to consider their particular protein requirements. To do this you will need to refer to the chart below (discussed in Chapter 2). If your horse has a protein requirement of between 7 and 8 per cent then most good quality feeds will provide this. If the demand is above 8.5 per cent then you may need to include a feed that is high in protein when selecting your horse's feeds.

Table 7.5 Protein requirements in the horse

Horse	Crude Protein level in % of diet
Maintenance	7.0–8.0
Light work	7.5–8.0
Medium work	8.0–9.0
Hard work	9.0–10.0
Fast work	9.5–10.0
Pregnancy: 9th month	8.9
Pregnancy: 10th month	9.0
Pregnancy: 11th month	9.5
Foal: first 3 months of lactation	12
Foal: next 3 months of lactation	10
Weanling	13
Yearling: 12–18 months	11
Yearling: 18–24 months	10
Yearling: 24–48 months	10

Adapted from Nutritional Requirements of Horses.

ENERGY AND PROTEIN REQUIREMENT FOR GROWTH

Foals and youngsters grow very rapidly in the first months of their life and this growth requires energy and protein.

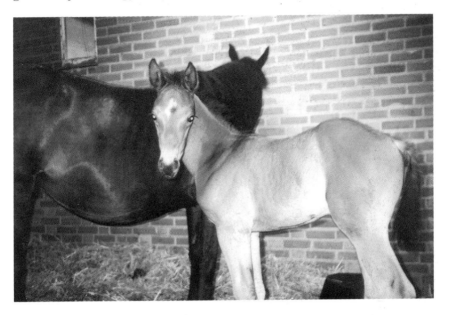

Youngstock need enough energy and protein to ensure they grow at the correct rate

The young horse should achieve 90 per cent of their mature weight by the time they are 12 months old but this is dependent on the correct nutrition. If a young horse is overfed they may grow too quickly and if underfed their growth rate will be slow. As a rough guide a Thoroughbred foal should weight 10 per cent of their adult weight.

A foal has different nutritional requirements to a yearling due to the different organs and structures that are growing and developing. The foal has a high demand for bone-forming minerals, vitamins and protein as the systems are forming and growing rapidly.

When the majority of these developments have occurred the foal's growth rate starts to slow down and the nutritional requirements alter. The young horse will now put energy into laying down muscle and fat and begin to fill out. At this time in their life they require a high carbohydrate level in the diet.

To minimise the risk of growth problems such as DOD it is necessary to maintain a gradual increase in growth, and therefore a gradual increase in nutrition.

Table 7.6 Daily nutritional requirement for youngstock

Age	Estimated weight (kg)	Daily gain (kg)	Total digestible energy MJDE	Crude protein in grams
6 months	200	0.30	32	376
	400	0.55	54	643
	500	0.65	63	750
	600	0.75	72	850
	700	0.80	85	1,001
12 months	200	0.20	37	392
	400	0.40	66	700
	500	0.50	80	851
	600	0.65	96	1,023
	700	0.70	110	1,176
18 months	200	0.10	35	375
	400	0.25	67	716
	500	0.35	83	893
	600	0.45	101	1,077
	700	0.50	114	1,215

Adapted from Nutritional Requirements of Horses.

ENERGY AND PROTEIN REQUIREMENTS FOR STUD STOCK

The mare

Broodmares have specific nutrient demands due to the demands put on the body when pregnant or lactating. Mares that are not in foal can be fed as a horse on a maintenance diet and it is important not to get barren mares too overweight as this can cause problems when trying to get them in foal.

The nutrition of a pregnant mare needs to be carefully considered as it has a direct effect on the survival, growth and development of the foetus. Studies have shown that correct nutrition in the 18th to 35th day of pregnancy assists in minimising the risk of reabsorption of the foetus.

A pregnant mare's nutritional requirements can be split into two parts: the first eight months of the pregnancy and the final three months before birth. During the first eight months of pregnancy the foetus goes through many cell changes but the growth rate is very small. A pregnant mare in the wild will be very vulnerable to predators if she is heavily pregnant so nature has devised a set-up which minimised this state to the last three months of an eleven-month pregnancy. As the foetus places little demand on the mare during this eight-month period, as long as she is in good condition she can be fed a maintenance diet. The aim in this period is to maintain her condition and ensure she receives a correct balance of all the required nutrients to prevent any deficiencies occurring.

The last three months of the pregnancy put a much greater demand on the nutrients being fed to the mare and these demands must be met if the mare and growing foetus are to remain healthy. **During these final three months the mare should be fed an addition of approximately 6 per cent of the maintenance requirement.** There is an added problem when feeding a pregnant mare that during the final three months they tend to lose their appetite. The large foetus puts pressure on the stomach and intestines, which restricts the capacity and gives the mare a false 'full' feeling. This means that the amount fed needs to be reduced and the number of feeds increased, so still providing the required amount but over a number of small feeds.

Table 7.7 Daily nutritional requirement for the pregnant mare

Horse	Maintenance energy requirement MJDE	Energy in final 3 months MJDE	Total concentrate ration in final 3 months	Total forage ration in final 3 months
200 kg	38	40	1–2 kg	2–3 kg
400 kg	58	61	4–6 kg	2–4 kg
500 kg	68	72	5–8 kg	3–5 kg
600 kg	78	83	6–9 kg	3–6 kg
700 kg	88	93	7–11 kg	4–7 kg

Adapted from Nutritional Requirements of Horses.

The lactating mare

Once the mare has given birth to a foal she now requires extra energy to feed the foal with milk and this lactation is more demanding on the mare than the pregnancy. Lactation requires a high level of energy. It is estimated that a mare can produce up to 5 per cent of her bodyweight in milk each day and foals suckle frequently so there must be a constant supply to fulfil the foal's appetite.

Energy requirements

The energy needed to produce this milk is equivalent to that used by a horse in hard work. The energy demand is between 50 and 75 per cent over maintenance because conversion of digested feeds into milk is not a very efficient process. Not only does the energy requirement increase substantially but also the protein, calcium, phosphorous and vitamin A requirements. If this nutrient demand is not met the mare will draw on her own reserves in order to provide for her foal and her condition will deteriorate. She will eventually use up her own nutrient stores leading to weakness and poor health. The foal will eventually suffer when the mare's own supply diminishes. This will show through poor growth rates and ill health.

These increased nutritional requirements are usually provided by the lush

The lactating mare needs plenty of energy to produce milk for her foal

spring grass, supplemented by a specific compound feed. Research has found that adding fat to the lactating mare's ration increased the fat content in the milk which increased the condition of their suckling foals. It also reduces the weight of the feeds as fat is a rich source of energy so less needs to be fed.

Protein requirements

The protein requirement for milk production alters over the first five days of lactation. The first milk produced, known as colostrum, is very rich in antibodies and vitamin A. This milk has a protein content of 19 per cent which drops to 8 per cent within 12 hours. Over a period of eight days this percentage drops even further to 2 per cent.

It would not be practical to alter the mare's diet this many times in order to accommodate these changes but it is essential to provide enough crude protein in the diet to enable the mare to produce this milk. Therefore a supply of 12–13 per cent crude protein is needed in the first three months of lactation which drops to 10–11 per cent for the rest of the period of lactation.

132

Table 7.8 Daily nutritional requirement for the lactating mare

Horse	Energy for first 3 months of lactation MJDE	Energy for final period of lacation MJDE	Crude protein first 3 months %	Crude protein next 3 months %
200 kg	66	57	12–13%	10–11%
400 kg	101	87	12–13%	10–11%
500 kg	119	102	12–13%	10–11%
600 kg	136	117	12–13%	10–11%
700 kg	154	132	12–13%	10–11%

Adapted from Nutritional Requirements of Horses.

Nutritional demands on the stallion

When a stallion is not covering mares he will require no more than the maintenance diet unless he is in work when the diet can be devised for a working horse. During the stud season the stallion's energy requirement will increase. This is due to the demands put on him when teasing and covering and to replace the energy lost through nervous energy as many stallions become much more fretful during the stud season and are more likely to lose condition through stress than from covering.

A stallion in good condition should be fed following the formula for a horse in light to medium work depending on how fretful they become. There should not be any need to give extra supplementation if the horse is healthy and in good condition. Some stallions are fed very little in the form of concentrate feeds even during the stud season, tending to perform better on a high roughage diet.

When feeding a stallion the aim is to maintain condition and ensure he receives a correct balance of all the standard nutrients needed by a mature horse. Research has shown that there is no evidence to support the need for extra supplementation to improve sperm production and fertility. The biggest problem that the stallion can suffer during the stud season is overfeeding leading to obesity. An overweight stallion is more likely to suffer decreased sex drive and impotency.

FEEDING THE UNDERWEIGHT HORSE

Before deciding what to feed the malnourished horse it is important to ascertain why the horse is underweight. Such a problem can be caused by numerous situations which include:

- Dental problems
- Disease
- Overgrazed pastures

The underweight horse needs to be fed up very gradually

- Poor quality feeds
- Incorrect feeding
- Worm burden or worm damage
- Neglect.

Once the reason for the malnourishment has been ascertained and the cause removed then the malnourishment can be dealt with.

It is essential when building up a thin horse to increase the feed very gradually as the horse's systems are likely to be unbalanced and if too much feed is introduced too quickly it is likely to cause colic. Initially the horse should be offered as much good quality hay as it can eat, plenty of fresh water and a mineral lick. Once the horse is eating adequate amounts of hay a probiotic supplement can be fed to help ensure that there are a balance of gut microbes available to ferment the roughage.

At this point a concentrate feed can also be added to the diet. The concentrate needs to have a good protein level (9–10 per cent) to enable the horse to repair and build up all the systems. The energy level needs to be between 10 and 11 MJDE per kg and the feed should contain conditioning ingredients such as barley, oil or sugarbeet. The horse should be offered the concentrate feed over three or four feeds, so they are getting very small amounts on a regular basis. This needs to be gradually built up over three or four weeks until the horse is on the amount required for the bodyweight.

It is important when building up a thin horse that they are kept warm and not worked too hard as most of the energy needs to go into building the horse's condition.

Supplementation may be necessary until the horse has returned to the correct weight. These horses are often lacking body fat so have very little fat tissue to store fat soluble vitamins, so a supplement that includes vitamins A, D, E and K can be fed.

FEEDING THE OLD HORSE

The older horse requires careful attention as their nutritional demands differ. As the horse reaches his twenties the following factors can start to have an effect on their diet:

- Wear and deterioration of the teeth
- Loss of teeth
- Elongation of the incisors
- Loss of weight and body condition
- Stiffness and loss of mobility in joints
- Impaired ability to digest and absorb feeds.

There are now specific compound feeds designed for the older horse that have a higher protein content, more digestible energy sources and higher levels of certain vitamins and minerals.

If the horse is prone to losing condition their standard ration may need to be increased by 10–20 per cent and a conditioning feed such as corn oil may be given. Some older horses can go the other way and become fatter as they grow old due to the lack of work and less activity. Being overweight can be as problematic as being underweight. It can predispose the horse to laminitis, arthritis and heart disease.

If the older horse is suffering from teeth problems he should be given feeds that are easy to eat such as processed grains and in severe cases mashes. Avoid any pellets or cubes and soak any hay as it will make it easier to chew.

FEEDING THE SICK HORSE

The diet of a sick or lame horse plays an important role in assisting the horse's body to recover and return to health. The body needs nutrients in order to fight infections, build up a strong immune system and repair damaged structures and tissues.

The convalescing horse has specific feed requirements in order to regain strength and make a quick recovery

The feed requirement of an ill horse increases but their appetite often decreases or goes completely and this can cause problems. Swallowing may be difficult for a sick horse and there may be digestive disturbances that can lead to dehydration and an electrolyte imbalance occurring. Therefore, when feeding a sick horse the aim is to minimise the loss of condition and tissue damage, maintain food intake and replenish any lost nutrients so that the body can fight the illness and effectively repair the damaged systems so that convalescence is reduced.

It is essential that the feeds chosen contain adequate amounts of energy (9–10 MJDE per kg) and protein that is of a high quality (containing essential amino acids such as lysine and methionine). The feed must contain a variety of vitamins and minerals and be tempting to encourage eating. It is very likely that a sick horse will be on box rest so do not overfeed the energy or protein as this can also cause problems such as filled legs and laminitis. You must fulfil the requirements but not overdose the systems.

Wet feeds such as sugarbeet and soaked hay can provide valuable fluids to a horse suffering from diarrhoea and dehydration.

If the horse has been on a course of antibiotics they may well benefit from B vitamin supplementation as the antibiotics will have killed the gut microflora which normally produce B vitamins. The addition of probiotics to replace the gut microflora will also be advantageous to the horse's digestive system.

The key points to remember when devising a diet for the sick horse are:

- Ensure it contains adequate energy to maintain condition.
- Ensure the protein is of a high quality, containing essential amino acids.
- Provide plenty of good quality soaked hay.
- Keep each feed very small.
- Offer the horse feeds at regular intervals and always discard any uneaten feed.
- Make the feeds tempting, adding fresh succulents and molasses or sugarbeet.
- Warm, cooked feeds can be tempting and are easy to digest if the horse is off his food or very ill.
- Keep the horse supplied with plenty of fresh water and carefully monitor the water intake.
- Consider feeding a vitamin, mineral and amino acid supplement to redress any deficiencies that occur during the illness and while convalescing.

CHAPTER 8
Selecting the Correct Feed

Once the energy and protein requirements for your horse have been ascertained, you need to decide which feed will supply these and the other essential nutrients. This can be the hardest aspect of feeding horses and is mainly due to the fact that there is so much to choose from. Being confronted by rows and rows of different sacks that all seem to do a similar job is enough to confuse the most experienced horse owner. This is where the feed calculations can help. Now you know what energy must be provided from the concentrate and forage part of the diet you simply have to select the feed that provides this and fulfils your horse's other nutrient requirements.

CHOOSING A CONCENTRATE FEED

Chapter 3 discussed the nutritional content of all the main feeds available to your horse and there is a wide selection to choose from. There is always a debate between feeding compound feeds, such as mixes, or straights, such as oats. If the diet is balanced then it is simply a case of personal preference as to which you choose but it is more difficult to ensure your horse receives a balanced diet when feeding straights because the nutritional value of each sack can alter, and the feed values are not stated on the sack. To make an informed choice you need to ask yourself a number of questions:

Does your horse have any specific nutritional requirements?
If your horse is growing, pregnant or lactating you will need to consider the protein content and select a feed that is rich in high quality proteins (refer to Chapter 3).

Does your horse need to put on weight or condition?
If so you will need to consider a feed that has conditioning qualities, for example, barley or conditioning mixes and cubes.

Does your horse suffer from any feed allergies?
If so you will need to ensure that you avoid them and it may be easier to feed straights than risk a cube or mix.

Are you feeding a number of horses at one time or just one or two horses?
Straights, once processed, for example, rolling or bruising will have a short shelf life of three weeks and you need to know they will be used up within this time. It

can be cheaper to bulk buy when feeding a number of horses and in this case compound feeds tend to last longer, unless you are purchasing whole oats and rolling them yourself prior to use.

How much storage space do you have?
If you have limited storage space then a compound feed may be more suitable than feeding two or three straights which take up more space.

What is your budget?
Compound feeds can be more expensive than straights, but you may need more than one straight feed which can increase the costs.

If you have decided on a compound feed you still have to narrow it down to which type and manufacturer. As can be seen on the nutritional tables in Chapter 3 each manufacturer's cool mix may have a different energy value and nutritional break-down so do not just assume that all quiet mixes are the same! When deciding upon a particular compound feed you should consider the following:

Do you want a mix or cube?
Cubes have a higher fibre content but are denser in weight so you get less volume per kilogram than a mix. Cubes can be more difficult to chew for older horses and some teething youngsters.

Do you want the feed to include any particular ingredients?
Some people like to feed a mix with additional herbs or that has a higher fat content for conditioning.

Is the feed manufacturer using a qualified nutritionist to design their feed and do they provide clear details as to exactly what the feed contains?
You will need information on the energy content in MJDE, the percentage of crude protein, fibre content and additional vitamins and minerals in order to design a balanced ration using this feed.

How fresh is the feed?
Ensure the feed is not close to or beyond the sell-by date which is printed on the sack or on the ingredients label.

Can anyone advise me?
Many of the larger manufacturers advertise a feed helpline which can be beneficial if you need any assistance.

By checking all these aspects it should narrow down your choice, the last step is to match your horse's specific dietary requirements with one of the feeds.

Table 8.1 Nutritional values of common feeds

Feed	MJDE/kg	Crude protein %	Oil %	Calcium g/kg	Phosphorous g/kg	Lysine g/kg
Oats	11	10	4.5	0.7	3.0	3.2
Naked oats	16	13.5	9.7	0.2	0.4	5
Barley	13	9.5	1.8	0.6	3.3	3.0
Maize	14	9.1	3.8	0.2	3.0	2.6
Sugarbeet	10	8	1.0	10	11	2.8
Linseed	18.5	30	32	2.4	5.2	7.7

Adapted from Horse Nutrition and Feeding *by Sarah Pilliner (1993).*

The nutritional values of the compound feeds are listed in the tables in Chapter 3.

Example feed choice

Our 16 hh, 517 kg horse is in medium work and needs 30 MJDE a day from the concentrate part of the feed. He has no specific problems and is in good condition. As the owners only have the one horse a compound feed is the most straightforward solution.

The maximum amount to be fed is 4 kg in weight and the energy provided needs to be 30 MJDE per day. Therefore the minimum energy level to look for is:

$$\frac{30 \text{ MJDE}}{4} = 7.5 \text{ MJDE per kg}$$

This gives us a wide choice as the following feeds fall into this category:

- Low energy feeds
- Herbal feeds
- High fibre feeds
- Medium work feeds.

As this horse is in good condition it is not necessary to feed to the maximum so 3.5 kg may be a better choice. This means using a feed that has an energy value of 8.5 MJDE per kg. By looking through the tables of compound feeds in Chapter 3 the following feeds fall into this category:

- Allen and Page quiet pencils
- Balanced Horse Feeds oatless mix.

To feed even less in weight and drop to 3 kg a day the energy level would increase to 9–10 MJ DE per kg so the compounds that could be fed are:

- Allen and Page herbal mix
- Baileys No 8

- Baileys horse and pony cubes
- Dodson and Horrell pasture mix.

This owner has decided on Dodson and Horrell pasture mix as she can feed 3 kg leaving up to 10 kg to be fed in hay and grass and wants a feed with additional herbs. To check this is the correct choice look on the feed sack or manufacturer's literature and note down the energy level in MJDE per kg. Then divide the energy requirement (30 MJDE a day) by the MJDE per kg in the feed (10 MJDE per kg) and it will tell you how much to feed which falls exactly into what we wanted to feed (3 kg a day). A compound feed contains the essential vitamins and minerals that this horse requires so no additional supplementation will be required.

CHOICE OF ROUGHAGES

This decision is not normally as complicated due to the fact that there is much less choice available. The choices tend to be:

- Meadow hay
- Seed hay
- Haylage
- Silage
- Alfalfa (lucerne).

The seasons and environment also affect this choice:

- In the winter many horses are stabled and so the forage requirement is greater.
- Many horses get turned out to grass for a period each day and this needs to be considered when deciding on a forage.
- If the horse has a dust allergy or is suffering from COPD (Chronic Obstructive Pulmonary Disease) then this will affect your decision.
- Horses in hard work need to gain more energy from the forage part of the ration than horses in light or medium work.

Example choice of roughages
Our example horse is stabled and in medium work. He suffers no allergies so the first choice would be a good quality meadow hay. This horse needs to gain 71 MJDE a day from the roughages and the maximum to be fed is 10 kg. The 71 MJDE divided by 10 gives a MJDE per kg of 7.1 and we need to be sure that meadow hay will provide this. The energy content of a good meadow hay usually falls into the range of 8–9 MJDE per kg so it will more than fulfil our horse's requirements.

PROTEIN REQUIREMENTS

Once the energy requirements of your horse have been decided, you now need to consider the protein requirements. The majority of good quality feeds have enough protein to fulfil a horse's requirements if in light to medium work. When the work increases or when a horse is growing or lactating this protein requirement may exceed the level provided in a standard diet and this needs to be checked and rectified if necessary.

To check the protein level you need to:

1. Check the protein content in each of the feeds (see summary charts in Chapter 3).
2. Multiply this figure by the amount in kilograms being fed, this will give the amount of protein in grams that each feed is supplying.
3. Add up all the grams of protein to give a total for the ration.
4. Divide the total grams of protein by the total kilograms of feed supplied and this will give the percentage of crude protein this diet is providing your horse.
5. Check this figure against the crude protein requirement of horses in Chapter 2 to see if it is adequate.
6. If the diet is providing too little then it will be necessary to reconsider your choice of feeds and start again with feeds that have a higher protein content.

Example diet

So far the selected feeds for our example horse are:

- 3 kg of Dodson and Horrell pasture mix per day.
- 10 kg of good quality meadow hay per day.

As the horse is being fed a compound feed and good quality hay it is very likely that the protein content will be sufficient but you should still check as it may even be too high for this particular horse.

The crude protein requirement for this horse is 8 per cent.

Feeds	Quantity		Protein content %		Protein in ration (g)
Mix	3 kg	x	9.5	=	28.5
Hay	10 kg	x	8	=	80
	13 kg				108.5 g

Therefore the percentage in the diet is: $$\frac{108.5}{13} \quad = \quad 8\%$$

So this feed supplies the exact amount of protein needed by this horse.

Alternative feed choice for the example horse

If we decided to feed this horse straight feeds instead of compound feeds the choice could be:

- Oats
- Naked oats
- Barley
- Chaff
- Sugarbeet.

As the horse is in medium work and in good condition, oats are the first choice as they provide a good source of energy but are not too fattening. It is very important when feeding any straight feeds that the calcium levels are considered as all the grains are deficient in calcium. A way of addressing this imbalance is to add sugarbeet to the ration as it is a very rich source of calcium. When using sugarbeet in a calculated ration the weight is always a *dry* weight before any water is added.

The oats have a feed value of 11 MJDE per kg; the sugarbeet has a feed value of 10 MJDE per kg. To obtain the correct balance of the weight of oats to sugarbeet is simply a method of trial and error, it may take many different combinations until the correct one is reached. For example:

Example A:

2.5 kg of oats will supply our example horse with   (11 x 2.5) 27.5 MJDE
0.5 kg of sugarbeet will supply the horse with   (10 x 0.5) 5 MJDE
This gives a total of 32.5 MJDE per day, which is just too high.

Example B:

1.5 kg of oats will supply the horse with   (1.5 x 11) 16.5 MJDE
1.5 kg of sugarbeet will supply the horse with   (1.5 x 10) 15 MJDE
This gives a total of 31.5 MJDE per day, which is slightly lower than example A.

So example B is closer to 30 MJDE per day that the horse requires. As it is 1.5 MJDE over the requirement you would need to keep a close eye on the horse to ensure that there is no weight gain or problems.

PROTEIN VALUES

Feeds	Quantity		Protein content %	Protein in ration (g)
Oats	1.5 kg	x	10	15
Sugarbeet	1.5 kg	x	8	12
Hay	10 kg	x	8	80
	13 kg			107 g

Therefore the percentage of crude protein in this diet is: $\dfrac{107}{13} = 8\%$

This is the exact level required by this horse.

DIET CHECKS

Once the feed has been chosen, you need to make certain checks and monitor your horse to ensure the feed is fulfilling the horse's individual requirements. The horse should not gain or lose condition if the diet is correct, unless that was one of your requirements. A check should be kept on the weight of your horse by eye, weigh-tape or a weighbridge and the necessary alterations made if required. The following questions should be asked:

Is the food satisfying the horse's appetite?
Even if you are supplying all the required nutrients the horse could still feel un-satisfied psychologically with a particular diet and could suffer cravings for roughage or demonstrate signs of boredom.

Is the horse eating up each feed and keen for the next?
If not you may be overfeeding and could need to cut down the amount. Or your feed may not be palatable and the quality should be checked.

What alterations may be necessary?
Your horse's diet needs to be altered regularly according to the work done and season. One diet plan will not be relevant for a whole year. You should devise at least two plans, one for summer and one for winter and ideally produce a new plan every time there is a change in the horse's requirements.

FEED CHOICES FOR YOUNGSTOCK

The foal
Many foals are introduced to a hard feed as the mare's milk begins to dwindle. The concentrates supplement the milk and enable the foal to become accustomed to eating hard feed before the stress of weaning.

The most common feed offered to foals during this period is a compound creep feed. These feeds are usually pelleted and are designed to provide the correct balance of nutrients for the foal. The creep feed will have a high protein level with adequate lysine and be rich in the minerals and vitamins required for growth. By three months old a foal should be eating about 0.5 kg for every 50 kg of body-weight, per day.

When weaned the foal can continue on the creep feed or gradually begin to change on to a different diet. If a diet of cereals is decided upon, then a supplement that contains at least 20 g of lysine and is rich in calcium must be fed as cereals are deficient in both these essential nutrients.

The yearling

The rate of growth of the yearling is slower than that of the weanling but they still have a higher demand for high quality protein, carbohydrates and minerals. The simplest feed to choose is a yearling cube or mix as it is nutritionally balanced so there is no worry about supplements. A cereal-based diet will still need supplementation of lysine and calcium, which can be provided by feeding soyameal, linseed, alfalfa or limestone flour with the grain. Youngstock should receive 1.25–1.6 kg of concentrates per 100 kg of bodyweight with an appropriate supplement when necessary.

FEEDING THE PREGNANT AND LACTATING MARE

Pregnancy

Adequate nutrition is essential to enable a mare to conceive and give birth to a healthy foal. Research has shown that mares that score 4–5 on condition scoring have the most successful conception rates and that the fatter a mare becomes the less likelihood there is of conceiving.

The first eight months of pregnancy put little demand on the nutritional requirements of the mare and they can be fed on a maintenance diet that holds condition but does not increase the bodyweight.

During the final three months of pregnancy the mare will need a feed that supplies a high quality protein. The crude protein demand is 10 per cent, which is not usually achieved in a standard diet. A compound stud feed can be fed or a diet of straights which includes a high quality protein feed such as soyameal, linseed or alfalfa.

The mare will also need to be given feeds that contain a high level of calcium, phosphorous and vitamin A. Examples of such feeds are sugarbeet, oils, limestone flour, dicalcium phosphate, milk powder and carrots. If a broodmare is over 10 years old she should be fed an extra 1 oz of calcium each day as her calcium absorption is less efficient than a younger mare.

When choosing a feed for the pregnant mare, weight as well as nutrient content should be considered. A heavily pregnant mare will have a smaller appetite and will not eat large feeds. It may be more sensible to feed small amounts of a high energy feed than larger amounts of a lower energy feed. If you choose to feed an oil to increase the energy levels you need to check the vitamin E provision. If feeding more than 3 per cent of oil in the diet you must increase the vitamin E by 5 mg/kg for each 1 per cent of oil over this 3 per cent level.

Lactation

The lactating mare has a very high demand for water, energy (100–130 MJDE per day) and protein (12–13 per cent) and very specific feeds are required to meet this. There are a number of compound feeds specifically designed for lactation or a variety of straights such as maize, naked oats, soyameal, corn oil, linseed oil and alfalfa can be used. When using straight feeds you must ensure that adequate levels of lysine, calcium, phosphorous, vitamin D and vitamin A are being provided. If feeding more than 3 per cent of oil in the diet you must check the vitamin E provision as an increase of 5 mg/kg of vitamin E should be added for each 1 per cent over this 3 per cent level.

FEEDING THE COMPETITION HORSE

Every discipline has differing feed requirements but they are all based on the same principles:

- To provide energy for the work done.
- To provide the required nutrients to maintain condition and health.
- To maintain fluid balance.
- To maintain the mineral and vitamin balance.

A horse that is competing regularly can be problematic to feed as they often go off their feed prior to or after an event. Fit horses that are in hard work have a high energy requirement and this can lead to the horse losing his appetite as he is faced with either large or frequent concentrate meals.

The one-day event horse

The event horse is one of the hardest horses to devise a balanced diet for as they need enough energy to see them through the cross-country and showjumping but need to be relaxed and calm in the dressage arena. Many riders have recently found that it is easier to achieve this by feeding higher levels of good quality roughage feeds and reducing the concentrate feeds.

Ideally the horse's diet should not alter before or after an event as sudden changes such as increasing concentrates or taking out ingredients can lead to digestive upsets. If a horse goes off his feed the night before the event or while

146

stabled at a competition the best solution is to reduce the amount of concentrates fed and add in more of the higher energy feeds like oil, milk pellets or maize.

On the day of a competition the horse should be fed his normal breakfast but ensure there is at least four hours gap before the cross-country. If your horse is competing later in the day he can be given a small haynet to keep him satisfied and it may be possible to fit in a concentrate feed between the dressage and showjumping providing there is at least two hours digestion time.

If competing in the summer or if your horse sweats heavily a close eye must be kept on the fluid intake. Offer fresh water on a regular basis throughout the day and check for signs of dehydration (pinching the skin). If you suspect the horse is dehydrated encourage him to drink and provide electrolytes in the feed or water.

If the horse has had a heavy day competing they may not cope with their usual evening feed. Offering two smaller feeds may tempt them to eat or alternatively feed a mash then give the normal feed later on.

The endurance horse

This discipline has very specific feed requirements due to the long distances ridden. The horse needs a diet that will provide energy which the horse can store to use during the ride. Incorrect feeding can lead to insufficient stores of energy and the horse becoming fatigued during a ride. The protein content must be considered to enable the horse to repair and replenish body tissues.

A fibre diet containing high quality roughage is often fed as roughage holds fluids and provides a slow release of energy which is useful for stamina. The endurance horse uses a vast amount of energy during a ride and this must be provided by the diet if the horse is not to lose condition and become fatigued.

The most effective way to encourage the horse to store energy is to feed a high fat diet. The fats are digested very efficiently and stimulate the body to use this as an energy source when working. By using the fats for energy this saves using the limited glucose reserves until the fat source has been depleted. Some endurance riders are now feeding up to 10–12 per cent of oil in the diet which equates to 2–3 pints of oil a day. This amount of oil provides the same amount of energy as 3–4 kg of oats but is much less bulky. The added advantage of feeding higher amounts of oil is that there is less of a risk of the horse fizzing up than there would be on this large amount of concentrate feed.

The fluid requirements of an endurance horse is another essential factor in the diet. Electrolytes are a valuable addition to the diet and should be provided regularly, two or three days prior to the ride and during the ride in water or sugarbeet water.

An electrolyte imbalance will often result in spasms of the diaphragm known as 'Thumps'.

SHOWJUMPING AND DRESSAGE

These disciplines require accuracy, obedience and power for relatively short periods of time. The dressage horse tends to carry more weight than a showjumper but both types of horse can be prone to losing condition as they compete frequently over a long competition season. The aim when feeding these horses is to provide enough energy to keep them fresh and holding condition but not to overfeed leading to fizziness or the horse becoming fat. Most showjumpers and dressage horses are fed a commercial competition mix or a diet based on oats and sugar-beet with a good quality meadow hay as roughage.

CHAPTER 9

Example Diets

This chapter contains a variety of diets for a range of horses in winter and summer. These examples are designed to provide you with a guide to the methods used when devising a diet but it is important to remember there are many other alternative feeds that can be used. The real test is how the horse is looking when being fed the particular diet. Science gives you the calculations to work from but it is essential that you use your own knowledge of your horse, your judgement and your eye!

Some points to remember when devising any diet are:

- The diet may require adjustment depending on how the horse is faring.
- Feed according to bodyweight.
- Feed by weight not scoops.
- Feed according to the work done.
- Always feed just under appetite to keep the horse keen on his feed.
- Feed plenty of roughage and use good quality roughages.
- Select your feeds so that they fulfil your horse's particular requirements.

WINTER DIETS

Case study 1: Oscar

Breed and type:	11 hh Welsh Section A gelding, aged 2 years old.
Environment:	Lives out.
Work done:	Not yet in work.
Special requirements:	Has a tendency to put on weight.

Factors to consider:

- Availability of grass
- Condition and weight pony is carrying
- Weather conditions
- The pony is still growing.

Bodyweight:	185 kg		
Appetite:	2.5% of bodyweight	=	5 kg total feed per day
Maintenance:	$\dfrac{185 + 18}{10}$	=	36.5 MJDE per day

'Oscar'

Workload:	None	
Energy for growth:	The maintenance energy is adequate to cover the energy needed for the growth as the total energy needed for this pony to ensure he grows correctly is 35 MJDE (see Chapter 7).	
Ratio of feeds:	Winter:	concentrates 5%
		roughages 95%
	Spring and summer:	100 % roughage

Roughage feeds

During the winter 95 per cent of the pony's feed is supplied by the forage there-fore the roughage must provide approximately 34.5 MJDE per day. Though the pony is living out there is very little nutrient value in the grass so it can be discounted from the calculations. A high roughage content will help Oscar keep warm as it releases a large amount of heat during digestion. This can be provided by:

Meadow hay:	8 MJDE per kg so you would feed	4–5 kg per day (3–4 flakes).
Oat straw:	6 MJDE per kg so you would feed	5–6 kg per day (6–7 flakes).

Concentrate feeds
During the winter 5 per cent of this pony's diet is supplied by the concentrate feed, therefore the concentrate feed must supply 2 MJDE a day. When selecting the feed the energy and protein values need to be considered. This pony needs a low energy feed which will provide adequate protein and calcium for correct growth. A cube or high fibre feed will be beneficial as it has a higher fibre content than a mix.

Some examples are:

Badminton horse and pony cubes:	8.75 MJDE per kg
Allen and Page quiet pencils:	8.5 MJDE per kg
Dengie Hi-Fi:	7 MJDE per kg.

Table 9.1 Winter diet for Oscar

Feed	Kg	MJDE per day	Crude protein %	Protein grams per day	Scoops per day
Dengie Hi-Fi	0.5	3.5	10.5	5.25	1 scoop
Meadow hay	4	32	7	28	3 sections
Limestone flour	70g	–	–	–	–
TOTALS	4.5	35.5	–	33.25	–

Protein content: $\frac{33.25}{4.5} = 7\%$

This protein content is low as the ideal would be 9–10 per cent. This could be increased by the addition of a protein supplement such as linseed or soya. In the spring and summer this would be supplied from the grass but in the winter you may need to supplement with a high protein feed.

Case study 2: Felix

Breed and type:	16.2 hh Warmblood gelding, aged 8 years old.
Environment:	Stabled at night in winter and out all the time in spring and summer.
Work done:	Working at elementary level dressage and works for an hour each day, 6 days a week.

151

'Felix'

Special requirements: Can be prone to putting on weight and get full of himself if fed a high energy feed.

Factors to consider:

- Condition and weight horse is carrying at the time.
- Weather conditions.
- Level of work done.
- Horse is fully clipped so needs energy to maintain warmth.

Bodyweight: 585 kg
Appetite: 2.5% of bodyweight   =   14 kg total feed per day
Maintenance: $\frac{585 + 18}{10}$ =   76.5 MJDE per day

Workload: $3.5 = \frac{585 \times 3.5}{50}$ =   41 MJDE per day

Total energy: 76.5 + 41   =   117.5 MJDE per day
Ratio of feeds: Winter: concentrates 30%
                                    roughages 70%

Roughage feeds

During the winter 70 per cent of Felix's feed is supplied by the roughage therefore the roughage must provide approximately 82 MJDE per day. Though Felix is turned out in the day the grass has virtually no feed value so can be discounted from the calculations. This can be provided by:

Meadow hay: 8 MJDE per kg so you would feed 11 kg per day.
Haylage: 12 MJDE per kg so you would feed 7 kg per day.

Concentrate feeds

During the winter 30 per cent of this horse's diet is supplied by the concentrate feed, therefore the concentrate feed must supply a minimum of 35.5 MJDE a day. When selecting the feed energy and protein values need to be considered. Felix needs a medium energy feed which will provide adequate protein.

Some examples are:

Allen and Page light competition mix: 12.5 MJDE per kg
Dodson and Horrell phase three: 12.75 MJDE per kg
Spillers original mix: 13.2 MJDE per kg
Dengie Alfa-A: 10 MJDE per kg.

Table 9.2 Winter diet for Felix

Feed	Kg	MJDE per day	Crude protein %	Protein grams per day	Scoops a day (approximate)
Light comp mix	2.25	28	14	31.5	2 scoops
Dengie Alfa-A	1	10	11.5	11.5	2 scoops
Meadow hay	10	80	7	70	10–11 sections
TOTALS	13.25	118	–	113	–

Protein content: $\dfrac{113}{13.25} = 8\%$

This protein content fulfils Felix's requirements.

Case study 3: Fleece

Breed and type: 16.1 hh Thoroughbred mare, 21 years old.
Environment: Stabled at night, out during the day.
Work done: Schooling and hacking with some competing at weekends.

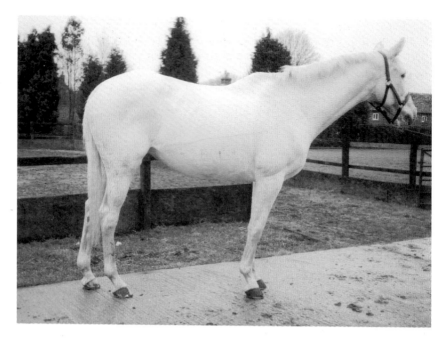

'Fleece'

Special requirements: Has tendency to lose weight in winter. Can become stiff in joints.

Bodyweight:	525 kg		
Appetite:	2.5% of bodyweight	=	13 kg total feed per day
Maintenance:	$\frac{525}{10} + 18$	=	70.5 MJDE per day
Workload:	$3 = \frac{525 \times 3}{50}$	=	31.5 MJDE per day
Total energy:	70.5 + 31.5	=	102 MJDE per day
Ratio of feeds:	Winter:		concentrates 25% roughages: 75%

Roughage feeds

During the winter 75 per cent of Fleece's feed is supplied by the roughage therefore the roughage must provide approximately 76.5 MJDE per day. This can be provided by:

Meadow hay:	8 MJDE per kg so you would feed 9.5 kg per day.
Haylage:	12 MJDE per kg, so you would feed 6 kg per day.

Concentrate feeds
During the winter 25 per cent of this horse's diet is supplied by the concentrate feed, therefore the concentrate feed must supply 25.5 MJDE per day. When selecting the feed energy and protein values need to be considered. Fleece needs a low–medium energy feed which will provide adequate protein. As she is old she needs a feed which will help keep her condition and be easy to eat, so a mix or straights may be preferable to a cube.

Some examples are:

Dengie Alfa-A:	10 MJDE per kg
Allen and Page old faithfuls mix:	11 MJDE per kg
Dodson and Horrell 16+:	11.5 MJDE per kg
Sugarbeet:	10 MJDE per kg
Oats:	11 MJDE per kg
Cooked flaked barley:	13 MJDE per kg.

Table 9.3 Winter diet for Fleece

Feed	Kg	MJDE per day	Crude protein %	Protein grams per day	Scoops a day (approximate)
D. and H. 16+ mix	1.25	14	13	16.25	1 scoop
Dengie Alfa-A	0.5	5	11.5	5.75	1 scoop
Sugarbeet	0.5	5	8	4	0.5 scoop dry
Meadow hay	9.75	78	7	68.25	8 sections
TOTALS	12	102	–	94.25	–

Protein content: $\dfrac{94.25}{12} = 8\%$

This protein content fulfils Fleece's requirements.

SUMMER DIETS

Case study 1: Jupiter

Breed and type:	15 hh three-quarter Thoroughbred gelding, 8 years old.
Environment:	Stabled. Out for a few hours a day due to lack of grass.
Work done:	Light work: mainly hacking three days a week and at weekends.
Special requirements:	Fretful temperament and has tendency to lose weight in winter.

155

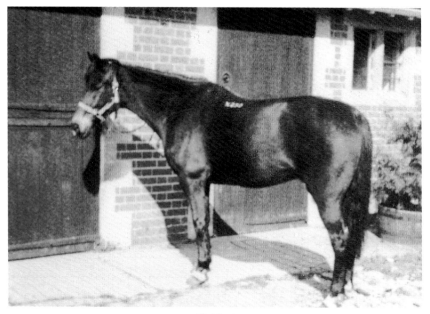

'Jupiter'

Bodyweight:	480 kg		
Appetite:	2.5% of bodyweight	=	12 kg total feed per day
Maintenance	$\frac{480 + 18}{10}$	=	66 MJDE per day
Workload	$2 = \frac{480 \times 2}{50}$	=	19 MJDE per day
Total energy:	66 + 19	=	85 MJDE per day
Ratio of feeds:	Winter:		concentrates 20% roughages 80%

Roughage feeds
During the summer 80 per cent of Jupiter's feed is supplied by the roughage therefore the roughage must provide approximately 68 MJDE per day. This can be provided by:

Meadow hay:	8 MJDE per kg so you would feed 8.5 kg per day.
Haylage:	12 MJDE per kg so you would feed 5.5 kg per day.

Concentrate feeds
During the winter 20 per cent of this horse's diet is supplied by the concentrate feed, therefore the concentrate feed must supply 17 MJDE a day. When selecting the feed energy and protein values must be considered. Jupiter needs a low

energy feed which will provide adequate protein and maintain his condition.

Some examples are:

Dengie Alfa-A:	10 MJDE per kg
Dengie Hi-Fi:	7 MJDE per kg
Allen and Page quiet pencils:	8 MJDE per kg
Allen and Page quiet mix:	9 MJDE per kg
BHF oatless mix:	8.5 MJDE per kg.

Table 9.4 Summer diet for Jupiter

Feed	Kg	MJDE per day	Crude protein %	Protein grams per day	Scoops a day (approximate)
Quiet pencils	1.5	12	10	15	1 scoop
Dengie Alfa-A	0.5	5	11.5	5.75	1 scoop
Meadow hay	8.5	68	7	63	7 sections
TOTALS	10.5	85	–	83.75	–

Protein content: $\dfrac{83.75}{10.5} = 8\%$

This protein content fulfils Jupiter's requirements.

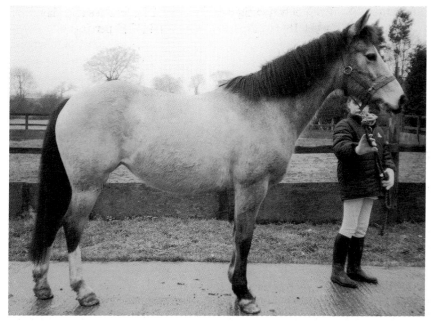

'Caramel'

157

Case study 2: Caramel

Breed and type:	14.1 hh Connemara mare, aged 12 years old.		
Environment:	Stabled at night, out during the day.		
Work done:	Light schooling and hacking each day and pony club events on some weekends.		
Special requirements:	Has tendency to put on weight.		
Bodyweight:	350 kg		
Appetite:	2.5% of bodyweight:	=	8.75 kg total feed per day
Maintenance:	$\frac{350}{10} + 18$	=	53 MJDE per day
Workload:	$2.5 = \frac{350}{50} \times 2.5$	=	17.5 MJDE per day
Total energy:	53 + 17.5		70.5. MJDE a day
Ratio of feeds:	Spring and summer:		concentrates 15% roughages 85%

Roughage feeds

During the spring and summer 85 per cent of Caramel's feed is supplied by the roughage therefore the roughage must provide approximately 59 MJDE per day. Some of this energy will be provided by the grass and unfortunately estimating how much grass is eaten is pure guesswork (refer to roughage chart)! A safe estimate to start with is that 50 per cent of the energy will be supplied by the grass. If the horse is leaving her hay or getting fat the hay ration may need to be cut down further. The aim is to provide 29.5 MJDE per day from the hay (50% of roughage energy). This can be provided by:

Meadow hay:	8 MJDE per kg so you would feed 3.5 kg per day.
Haylage:	12 MJDE per kg, so you would feed 2.5 kg per day.

Concentrate feeds

The concentrate feed supplies 15 per cent of this horse's diet, therefore the concentrate feed must supply 10.5 MJDE a day. When selecting the feed energy and protein values must be considered. Caramel needs a low energy feed which will provide adequate protein.

Some examples are:

Dengie Hi-Fi:	7 MJDE per kg
Allen and Page quiet mix:	9 MJDE per kg
BHF oatless mix:	8.5 MJDE per kg
Dodson and Horrell pasture mix:	10 MJDE per kg.

Table 9.5 Summer diet for Caramel

Feed	Kg	MJDE per day	Crude protein %	Protein grams per day	Scoops a day (approximate)
Quiet mix	0.5	4.5	10	5	0.5 scoop
Dengie Hi-Fi	0.5	3.5	10.5	5.25	1 scoop
Meadow hay	4	32	7	28	3–4 sections
Grass (estimated)	3	unknown	4	15	–
TOTALS	8	40	–	53.25	–

Protein content: $\dfrac{53.25}{8} = 7\%$

This protein content fulfils Caramel's requirements.

Case study 3: Felix

Breed and type: 16.2 hh Warmblood gelding, aged 8 years old.
Environment: Living out all the time in the spring and summer.
Work done: Working at elementary level dressage and works for a hour each day, 6 days a week. Competing once a fortnight.
Special requirements: Can be prone to putting on weight and can get full of himself if given a high energy feed.

Bodyweight: 585 kg
Appetite: 2.5% of bodyweight = 14 kg total feed per day
Maintenance: $\dfrac{585}{10} + 18$ = 76.5 MJDE per day
Workload: $3.5 = \dfrac{585 \times 3.5}{50}$ = 41 MJDE per day
Total energy: 76.5 + 41 = 117.5 MJDE per day
Ratio of feeds: Spring and summer: concentrates 30%
roughages 70%

Roughage feeds
During the spring 70 per cent of Felix's feed is supplied by the roughage therefore the roughage must provide approximately 82 MJDE per day. As Felix is living out all this roughage will be provided by the grass so there is no need to feed additional hay.

Concentrate feeds
The concentrate feed supplies 30 per cent of this horse's diet, therefore the concentrate feed must supply a minimum of 35.5 MJDE a day. When selecting the feed

'Felix'

energy and protein values must be considered. Felix needs a medium energy feed which will provide adequate protein.

Some examples are:

Allen and Page light competition mix: 12.5 MJDE per kg
Dodson and Horrell phase three: 12.75 MJDE per kg
Spillers original mix: 13.2 MJDE per kg
Dengie Alfa-A: 10 MJDE per kg.

Table 9.6 Summer diet for Felix

Feed	Kg	MJDE per day	Crude protein %	Protein grams per day	Scoops a day (approximate)
Light comp mix	3.25	40.5	14	45.5	2.5 scoops
Dengie Alfa-A	1.5	15	11.5	17.25	1.5 scoop
Grass (estimated)	10.25	59	4	47	–
TOTALS	15	114.5	–	109.75	–

'Ryan'

As the energy content of the grass is estimated the horse must be watched to ensure he does not begin to put on weight or have excess energy. If this occurs the concentrate feed should be cut down.

Protein content: $\dfrac{109.75}{15} = 7\%$

Case study 4: Ryan

Breed and type:	14.1 hh Welsh Cob gelding, 9 years old.		
Environment:	Stabled at night, out during the day.		
Work done:	Schooling each day and hacking at weekends.		
Special requirements:	Has tendency to put on weight.		
Bodyweight:	425 kg		
Appetite:	2.5% of bodyweight	=	11 kg total feed per day
Maintenance:	$\dfrac{425}{10} + 18$	=	60.5 MJDE per day
Workload:	$3 = \dfrac{425 \times 3}{50}$	=	25.5 MJDE per day
Total energy:	60.5 + 25.5	=	86 MJDE a day
Ratio of feeds:	Spring and summer:		concentrates 15% roughages 85%

Roughage feeds

During the spring and summer 85 per cent of Ryan's feed is supplied by the roughage therefore the roughage must provide approximately 73 MJDE per day. Some of this energy will be provided by the grass and unfortunately estimating how much energy the grass provides is pure guesswork! A safe estimate to start with is that 50 per cent will be supplied in the grass. If the horse is leaving his hay or is getting fat the hay ration may need to be cut down further. The aim is to provide 36.5 MJDE per day from the hay (50 per cent of roughage energy). This can be provided by:

Meadow hay:	8 MJDE per kg so you would feed 4.5 kg per day.
Haylage:	12 MJDE per kg so you would feed 3 kg per day.

Concentrate feeds

The concentrate feed supplies 15 per cent of this horse's diet, therefore the concentrate feed must supply 13 MJDE a day. When selecting the feed energy and protein values must be considered. Ryan needs a low energy feed which will provide adequate protein.

Some examples are:

Dengie Hi-Fi:	10 MJDE per kg
Allen and Page quiet mix:	9 MJDE per kg
Spillers pony cubes:	10 MJDE per kg
Dodson and Horrell pasture mix:	10 MJDE per kg
Spillers cool mix:	11.5 MJDE per kg.

Table 9.7 Summer diet for Ryan

Feed	Kg	MJDE per day	Crude protein %	Protein grams per day	Scoops a day (approximate)
Cool mix	0.75	8.62	11	8.25	–
Dengie Alfa-A	0.5	5	11.5	5.75	1 scoop
Meadow hay	4.5	36	7	31.5	3–4 sections
Grass (estimated)	4	unknown	5	20	–
TOTALS	10	50.5	–	65.5	–

Protein content: $\frac{65.5}{10} = 6.5\%$

This protein content is a fraction too low as the ideal would be 7–8 per cent. As Ryan is no longer growing and is in light to medium work it is unlikely to cause a problem but it is an area that will need to be monitored. Should you wish to increase the protein content, the diet could be supplemented with a high protein feed such as linseed oil or soyameal.

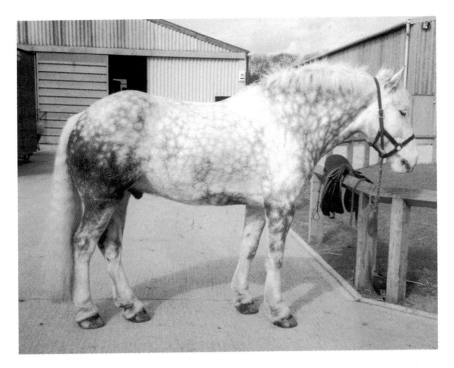

'Henry'

Case study 5: Henry

Breed and type:	16.1 hh Irish Draught gelding, aged 9 years old.
Environment:	Stabled at night and out in the day for a few hours.
Work done:	Worked for approximately 2 hours a day, schooling 6 days a week.
Special requirements:	Can be prone to putting on weight and tends to be lazy.

Bodyweight: 670 kg

Appetite: 2.5% of bodyweight = 17 kg total feed per day

Maintenance: $\dfrac{670 + 18}{10}$ = 85 MJDE per day

Workload: $3.5 = \dfrac{670}{50} \times 3.5$ = 47 MJDE per day

Total energy: 85 + 47 = 132 MJDE a day

Ratio of feeds: Summer: concentrates 25%
roughage 75%

Roughage feeds

Roughage supplies 75 per cent of Henry's feed, therefore the roughage must provide approximately 99 MJDE per day. Though Henry is turned out for a few hours a day the grass will provide only a little energy and protein so it can be discounted from the calculations. The roughage can be provided by:

Meadow hay: 8 MJDE per kg so you would feed 12 kg per day.
Haylage: 12 MJDE per kg so you would feed 8 kg per day.

Concentrate feeds

The concentrate feed supplies 25 per cent of this horse's diet, therefore the concentrate feed must supply 33 MJDE per day. When selecting the feed energy and protein values must be considered. Henry needs an average energy feed which will provide adequate protein.

Some examples are:

Allen and Page light competition mix: 12.5 MJDE per kg
Badminton hunter event cubes: 11 MJDE per kg
Spillers original mix: 13.2 MJDE per kg
Dengie Alfa-A: 10 MJDE per kg
Oats: 11 MJDE per kg.

Table 9.8 Summer diet for Henry

Feed	Kg	MJDE per day	Crude protein %	Protein grams per day	Scoops a day (approximate)
Oats	2	22	10	20	2.5 scoops
Dengie Alfa-A	1	10	11.5	11.5	2 scoops
Meadow hay	12.5	100	7	87.5	10–11 sections
TOTALS	15.5	132	–	119	–

Protein content: $\dfrac{119}{15.5}$ = 7.5 %

This protein content fulfils Henry's requirements.

THE BROODMARE

Factors to consider when feeding stud stock:

- Keep a close check on the condition and growth rate of the horses to avoid deficiencies or overfeeding.

- Only use good quality feeds.
- Ensure the horse is getting all the vitamins and minerals it requires from the feed.
- Feed little and often as heavily pregnant mares often go off their food due to the pressure from the foal on the stomach and intestine.

Example: Ella
A 15.3 hh Thoroughbred broodmare who is in the final 3 months of pregnancy.

'Ella'

Bodyweight:	500 kg
Appetite: at 3%	15 kg
Maintenance requirements:	68 MJDE per day
Additional energy requirements:	52 MJDE per day
Total energy requirement:	120 MJDE per day
Ratio of feeds:	concentrates 25%
	roughages 75%

Roughage feeds

Roughage supplies 75% of this horse's feed, therefore the roughage must provide approximately 90 MJDE per day. The roughage can be provided by:

Good meadow hay: 9 MJDE per kg
Seed hay: 10 MJDE per kg
Haylage: 12 MJDE per kg.

Concentrate feeds

Concentrate feed supplies 25 per cent of this horse's diet, therefore the concentrate feed must supply a minimum of 30 MJDE a day. When selecting the feed energy and protein values must be considered. An in-foal mare in the final three months of pregnancy needs 11 per cent protein and has a high requirement for calcium, phosphorous and vitamin A.

Some examples of concentrate feeds are:

Spillers breeding mix: 13.6 MJDE per kg
Dodson and Horrell stud diet: 12.8 MJDE per kg
Bailey's stud mix: 12.5 MJDE per kg
Dengie Alfa-A: 10 MJDE per kg.

Table 9.9 Diet for Ella

Feed	Kg	MJDE per day	Crude protein %	Protein grams per day
Breeding mix	3	40.8	16	48
Alfa-A	1.5	15	11.5	17.25
Good meadow hay	9	81	8	72
Limestone flour	90g	–	–	–
TOTALS	13.5	136.8	–	137.25

Protein content: $\dfrac{137.25}{13.5} = 10\%$

This protein content fulfils the horse's requirements.

THE LACTATING MARE

The lactating mare has an energy requirement that is equivalent to a three-day eventer. When feeding her foal the mare must be given enough energy and protein to provide the foal with adequate amounts of milk and maintain her condition.

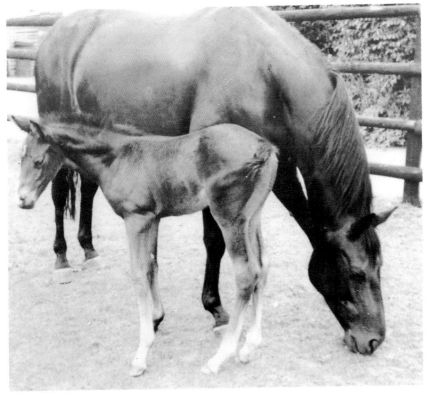

'Harriet'

Example: Harriet

A 15.3 hh part Thoroughbred broodmare.

Bodyweight:	500 kg
Appetite:	12 kg
Maintenance requirements:	68 MJDE per day
Additional energy requirements:	72 MJDE per day
Total energy requirement:	140 MJDE per day
Ratio of feeds:	concentrates 45%
	roughage 55%

Roughage feeds
Roughage supplies 55 per cent of this mare's feed, therefore the roughage must provide approximately 77 MJDE per day. The roughage can be provided by:

Good meadow hay:	9 MJDE per kg
Seed hay:	10 MJDE per kg
Haylage:	12 MJDE per kg.

Concentrate feeds

Concentrate feed supplies 45 per cent of this horse's diet, therefore the concentrate feed must supply a minimum of 63 MJDE a day. When selecting the feed energy and protein values must be considered. A lactating mare needs 12.5 per cent protein and has a high requirement for calcium, phosphorous and vitamin A.

Some examples of concentrate feeds are:

Spillers breeding mix:	13.6 MJDE per kg
Dodson and Horrell stud diet:	12.8 MJDE per kg
Bailey's stud mix:	12.5 MJDE per kg
Dengie Alfa-A:	10 MJDE per kg
Allen and Page stud pencils:	12.5 MJDE per kg
Corn oil:	35 MJDE per kg.

Table 9.10 Diet fot Harriet

Feed	Kg	MJDE per day	Crude protein %	Protein grams per day
Stud pencils	2.5	31.25	17	42.5
Alfa-A	1	10	11.5	11.5
Haylage	8	80	12	96
Limestone flour	90g	–	–	–
Corn oil	0.5	17.5	–	–
TOTALS	12	138.75	–	150

Protein content: $\frac{150}{12} = 12.5\%$

This protein content is sufficient for the mare.

THE YEARLING

Correct feeding of a yearling is essential if the horse is to grow at the correct rate and build strong bones and tissues.

Example

Estimated bodyweight when full grown:	500 kg
Appetite:	8 kg
Maintenance requirements:	68 MJDE per day
Additional energy requirements:	12 MJDE per day
Total energy requirement:	80 MJDE per day
Ratio of feeds:	concentrates 45%
	roughage 55%

The yearling

Roughage feeds

Yearlings should have access to a large amount of good quality herbage in order to maximise their nutrient intake and provide a good base for growth and development. If you do not have access to acres of good pasture land then you will have to supplement with other roughage feeds. This will also be the case in the winter. This roughage can be provided by:

Good meadow hay:	9 MJDE per kg
Seed hay:	10 MJDE per kg
Haylage:	12 MJDE per kg.

Concentrate feeds

Concentrate feed supplies 45 per cent of the yearling's diet. This feed ensures that the horse gets all the nutrients required, especially as the grass quality and quantity can vary dramatically. The concentrate feed in this diet must supply a minimum of 36 MJDE per day. When selecting the feed energy and protein values must be considered. A yearling needs 11–13.5 per cent protein (high demand) and has a high requirement for calcium, phosphorous and vitamin A.

Some examples of concentrate feeds that can achieve these requirements are:

Spillers yearling pellets:	13.4 MJDE per kg
Badminton foal pellets:	12 MJDE per kg

169

Bailey's foal starter: 13.5 MJDE per kg
Dengie Alfa-A: 10 MJDE per kg
Allen and Page foal pellets: 13 MJDE per kg
Corn oil: 35 MJDE per kg
Linseed oil: 18.5 MJDE per kg.

Table 9.11 Diet for a yearling during the winter

Feed	Kg	MJDE per day	Crude protein %	Protein grams per day
Allen and Page foal pellets	2.5	30	18.5	46.25
Alfa-A	1	10	11.5	11.5
Limestone flour	95 g	–	–	–
Milk powder	0.20	3.6	36	7.2
Good hay	3.5	35	10	35
TOTALS	7.2	78.6	–	99.95

Protein content: $\dfrac{99.95}{7.2} = 13.8\%$

This protein content is sufficient for the yearling.

COMPETITION HORSE DIETS

Factors to consider:

- Adequate energy for stamina and performance must be provided.
- Adequate protein to enable the horse to build muscle and repair damaged tissues must be provided.
- Condition must be maintained throughout the competition season.

The dressage horse

The dressage horse needs enough energy to enable them to cope with the demands of the test but not too much, otherwise they may blow up in the arena!

Example dressage horse

A 16.2 hh Warmblood working at advanced level, aged 10 years old. Stabled and suffers from a dust allergy.

Bodyweight: 590 kg
Appetite: 15 kg

Dressage horse

Maintenance requirements: 77 MJDE per day
Work score: 4.5
Performance requirements: 53 MJDE per day
Total energy requirement: 130 MJDE per day
Ratio of feeds: concentrates 30%
                            roughage 70%

Roughage feeds
Roughage supplies 70 per cent of this dressage horse's feed, therefore the roughage must provide approximately 91 MJDE per day. This can be provided by:

Meadow hay: 8 MJDE per kg
Seed hay: 10 MJDE per kg
Haylage: 12 MJDE per kg.

Concentrate feeds

Concentrate feed supplies 30 per cent of this horse's diet, therefore the concentrate feed must supply a minimum of 39 MJDE a day. When selecting the feed energy and protein values must be considered.

Some examples of concentrate feeds are:

Bailey's top line cubes:	13.5 MJDE per kg
BHF high performance mix:	13 MJDE per kg
Burgess supa horse:	15 MJDE per kg
Spillers high performance mix:	14 MJDE per kg
Oats:	11 MJDE per kg
Dengie Alfa-A:	10 MJDE per kg.

Table 9.12 Diet for example dressage horse

Feed	Kg	MJDE per day	Crude protein %	Protein grams per day
High performance mix	2.5	35	13	32.5
Alfa-A	1.5	15	11.5	17.25
Meadow hay	9	72	7	63
Corn oil	0.25	8.75	–	–
TOTALS	13.25	130	–	112.75

Protein content: $\dfrac{112.75}{13.25} = 8.5\%$

This protein content fulfils the requirements.

The one-day event horse

The novice one-day event horse needs enough energy to enable him to cope with the demands of the cross-country and showjumping but stay calm enough for the dressage. They need to be fit, which can lead to a loss of appetite so the feeds need to be small but fulfil the energy requirements. During the competition season many horses lose condition or fret the weight off so this needs to be considered when planning the diet. If the weather is hot you also need to bear in mind the fluid and electrolyte balance to avoid dehydration.

Example novice event horse

A 15.2 hh Thoroughbred mare working at British Horse Society novice level, aged 11 years old. Stabled, turned out for a couple of hours a day.

Bodyweight:	510 kg
Appetite:	13 kg

The one-day event horse

Maintenance requirements: 69 MJDE per day
Work score: 5
Performance requirements: 51 MJDE per day
Total energy requirement: 120 MJDE per day
Ratio of feeds: concentrates 35%
                                 roughage 65%

Roughage feeds
Roughage supplies 65 per cent of this event horse's feed, therefore the roughage must provide approximately 78 MJDE per day. This can be provided by:

Meadow hay: 8 MJDE per kg
Seed hay: 10 MJDE per kg
Haylage: 12 MJDE per kg.

Concentrate feeds
Concentrate feed supplies 35 per cent of this horse's diet, therefore the concentrate feed must supply a minimum of 42 MJDE a day. When selecting the feed energy and protein values must be considered.

Some examples of concentrate feeds are:

Bailey's top line cubes: 13.5 MJDE per kg
BHF high performance mix: 13 MJDE per kg

173

Spillers original mix: 13.2 MJDE per kg
Burgess supa horse: 15 MJDE per kg
Oats: 11 MJDE per kg
Dengie Alfa-A: 10 MJDE per kg.

Table 9.13 Diet for example event horse

Feed	Kg	MJDE per day	Crude protein %	Protein grams per day
Spillers original mix	2	26.4	11	22
Alfa-A	1.5	15	11.5	17.25
Good meadow hay	8.	80	8	64
TOTALS	11.5	121	–	103.25

Protein content: $\dfrac{103.25}{11.5} = 9\%$

This protein content fulfils the requirements of this horse.

The showjumper

The showjumper

A showjumper uses a large amount of energy when propelling himself over fences and needs to jump at speed if jumping against the clock.

Example showjumping horse

A 16 hh Thoroughbred working at Foxhunter level, aged 6 years old. Stabled, turned out for a few hours each day.

Bodyweight:	530 kg
Appetite:	14 kg
Maintenance requirements:	71 MJDE per day
Work score:	4
Performance requirements:	42 MJDE per day
Total energy requirement:	113 MJDE per day
Ratio of feeds:	concentrates 35%
	roughage 65%

Roughage feeds

Roughage supplies 65 per cent of this horse's feed, therefore the roughage must provide approximately 73 MJ DE per day. This can be provided by:

Meadow hay:	8 MJDE per kg
Seed hay:	10 MJDE per kg
Haylage:	12 MJDE per kg.

Concentrate feeds

Concentrate feed supplies 35 per cent of this horse's feed, therefore the concentrate feed must provide a minimum of 40 MJDE per day. When selecting the feed energy and protein values must be considered.

Some examples of concentrate feeds are:

Dodson and Horrell phase 3:	12.75 MJDE per kg
BHF high performance mix:	13 MJDE per kg
Spillers high performance mix:	14 MJDE per kg
Oats:	11 MJDE per kg
Dengie Alfa-A:	10 MJDE per kg.

Table 9.14 Diet for example showjumping horse

Feed	Kg	MJDE per day	Crude protein %	Protein grams per day
D & H phase 3	2	25.5	13	26
Alfa-A	1.5	15	11.5	17.25
Meadow Hay	8	72	7	56
TOTALS	11.5	112.5	–	99.25

Protein content: $\dfrac{99.25}{11.5} = 8.5\%$

This protein content fulfils the horse's requirements.

The show pony

The show pony needs to have a good covering and be in top condition but maintain control in the show ring.

The show pony

Example show pony
A 14.2 hh part Arab gelding, aged 9 years old: stabled.

Bodyweight:	410 kg
Appetite:	10 kg
Maintenance requirements:	59 MJDE per day
Work score:	3.5
Performance requirements:	29 MJDE per day
Total energy requirement:	88 MJDE per day
Ratio of feeds:	concentrates 25 %
	roughage 75%

Roughage feeds
Roughage supplies 75 per cent of this horse's feed, therefore the roughage must provide approximately 66 MJDE per day. This can be provided by:

Meadow hay:	8 MJDE per kg
Seed hay:	10 MJDE per kg
Haylage:	12 MJDE per kg.

Concentrate feeds
Concentrate feed supplies 25 per cent of this horse's diet, therefore the concentrate feed must supply a minimum of 22 MJDE a day. When selecting the feed energy and protein values must be considered.

Some examples of concentrate feeds are:

Allen and Page show special mix:	10.75 MJDE per kg
BHF show mix: 1	0 MJDE per kg
Spillers conditioning cubes:	13.4 MJDE per kg
Cooked flaked barley:	13 MJDE per kg
Dengie Alfa-A:	10 MJDE per kg
Sugarbeet:	10 MJDE per kg
Corn oil:	35 MJDE per kg.

Table 9.15 Diet for example show pony

Feed	Kg	MJDE per day	Crude protein %	Protein grams per day
Show mix special	1.5	16	14	21
Alfa-A	1	10	11.5	11.5
Corn oil	0.25	8.75	–	–
Meadow hay	7	56	7	49
TOTALS	9.75	90	–	81.5

Protein content: $\dfrac{81.5}{9.75} = 8\%$

This protein content fulfils the horse's requirements.

The endurance horse

Endurance riding has grown in popularity over the past few years. Endurance horses require a very stringent training programme to prepare them for the 100-mile competitive rides involving 25 miles a day and their diet plays an essential part in this training. The majority of endurance horses are kept out during the day and stabled at night.

The endurance horse needs a very specialised diet. They have to make effective use of the energy that is fed in order to have the stamina to make the distance required of them. They should be fed adequate amounts of quality roughages as they hold water in the intestines which reduces the risk of dehydration. When working over more than 7 miles the endurance horse needs a high fat diet as the stores of body fat are a more effective source of energy than glucose. They also require a high fluid intake and need to be fed electrolytes two days before a ride, during a ride and the day after the ride to replace those lost in the sweat.

Example endurance horse

A 14.3 hh Arab mare, aged 9 years old. Stabled and turned out for a few hours a day. Competing at bronze horseshoe level.

Bodyweight:	420 kg
Appetite:	10 kg
Maintenance requirements:	60 MJDE per day
Work score:	5
Performance requirements:	42 MJDE per day
Total energy requirement:	102 MJDE per day
Ratio of feeds:	concentrates 35%
	roughage 65%

The endurance horse

Roughage feeds

Roughage supplies 65 per cent of this horse's feed, therefore the roughage must provide approximately 66 MJDE per day. The roughage can be provided by:

Meadow hay:	8 MJDE per kg
Seed hay:	10 MJDE per kg
Haylage:	12 MJDE per kg.

Concentrate feeds

Concentrate feed supplies 35 per cent of this horse's diet, therefore the concentrate feed must supply a minimum of 36 MJDE a day. When selecting the feed energy and protein values must be considered.

Some examples of concentrate feeds are:

Dodson and Horrell phase 3:	12.75 MJDE per kg
Spillers HDF cubes:	12.5 MJDE per kg
Spillers high performance mix:	14 MJDE per kg
Oats:	11 MJDE per kg
Dengie Alfa-A:	10 MJDE per kg
Corn oil:	35 MJDE per kg.

Table 9.16 Diet for example endurance horse

Feed	Kg	MJDE per day	Crude protein %	Protein grams per day
Spillers HDF cubes	2	25	13	26
Alfa-A	1.5	15	11.5	17.25
Corn oil	0.25	8.75	–	–
Haylage	7	56	7	49
TOTALS	10	104	–	92.25

Protein content: $\dfrac{92.25}{10} = 9\%$

This protein content fulfils the horse's requirements.

CHAPTER 10

Supplementing the Diet

WHAT IS A SUPPLEMENT

A supplement is simply a substance that can be added to a horse's diet to balance deficiencies. They are not miracle cures that can turn your horse into a grade A showjumper overnight and it is not the case that the more supplements you feed the better and healthier your horse will be! Many horse's survive in the best of health with no additional supplements, just a well balanced diet and some loving care!

There are very many supplements available ranging from the basic salt lick to a fully comprehensive mineral and vitamin mix containing a whole host of ingredients. The most common supplements purchased are: mineral supplements, vitamin supplements and protein supplements.

Common supplements fed in the diet

Supplements can also increase the nutrient content of a balanced diet if that diet is not supplying all the horse's requirements. Examples are probiotics and enzymes. These are fed for health reasons rather than to balance a diet.

Supplementing a horse's diet needs some careful thought and consideration. Supplements are readily available and there is a vast array to choose from but their action and use is often not fully appreciated or understood. The proper use of supplementation can improve the health and performance of a horse if the reason for the problem was a dietary deficiency but a healthy horse that is on a balanced diet is very unlikely to require any added extras. In fact overfeeding a supplement to a healthy horse can actually decrease performance and lead to ill health.

Before deciding to supplement one needs to consider the individual horse and its particular situation. Certain horses do have a higher requirement for nutrients and it is these horses that may benefit from supplementation. Such horses are: pregnant or lactating broodmares, youngsters, older horses, stabled performance horses and those receiving a diet based on hay and grains.

Below are some questions that can assist you when deciding if your horse requires supplementation:

Questions	Need for supplements?
What is horse being fed?	
Compound feeds	unlikely
Straights	likely
What is the environment?	
Fully stabled	likely
On good grass	unlikely
On poor grass	possible
What age?	
Youngster	likely
Pregnant	likely
Lactating mare	likely
Adult horse	unlikely
Elderly horse	likely
Work done?	
Hard work	possible
Stressful work	likely
Light work	unlikely
Off work	unlikely
State of health?	
Good	unlikely
Poor	likely
Recuperating	likely

Where the horse lives can mean that it will require a supplement, especially if it is living out or you cut your own hay. Certain areas of the country have soil deficiencies such as selenium. As a horse owner you can find out about soil deficiencies from ADAS or have a soil analysis carried out.

FEEDING A SUPPLEMENT

It is essential when feeding a supplement that you choose the correct one. Any supplement fed needs to supply what the horse is lacking but not oversupply the horse with other nutrients. As mentioned earlier, this can cause as many problems as not feeding the supplement at all.

There is a vast range of supplements on the market which range from the simple to the complex broad spectrum supplement and it is easy to be overwhelmed by the choice available. This decision can be made much easier by being aware of why the diet is being supplemented and which nutrients you need to supplement. Just because a supplement is of the expensive complex type this does not mean that it will contain the nutrients your horse needs. The selecting of the correct supplement is vital if it is to redress an imbalance.

SELECTING A SUPPLEMENT

Before purchasing a supplement there are some areas that should be investigated or considered. If you feel your horse is suffering from a specific nutritional deficiency then ask your vet to take a blood test. The vet can then advise on your horse's specific requirements.

If you are looking for a general feed supplement to balance the diet you should:

1. Check the nutritional content of your horse's usual feed.
   - If using a compound feed write down the vitamin and mineral levels and how much you are feeding per day.
   - If using a compound feed to the level that the manufacturer recommends then it is very unlikely that you will need to feed any of the vitamins and minerals already added to the feed.
   - If feeding straights you need to think about possible deficiencies such as calcium especially if the diet is not being supplemented at all.
2. Check the nutritional content of any supplements already being fed to ensure there is no overfeeding of certain nutrients.
3. Refer to the tables in the appendix on the daily recommended amounts of the vitamins and minerals for your horse and note down any that are not provided by your present feed.

4.   Select the supplements you feel are suitable and then check the ingredients. When selecting the supplements check:
   • It is produced by a reputable manufacturer who has carried out controlled trials and researched the effects of the supplement on a variety of horses.
   • That it contains a list of all the nutrients and give an amount and ideally a RDA.
   • If the RDA is not stated it is worth finding out what the RDA is and then comparing it to each supplement.
   • That its dose is based on the weight of the horse rather than by scoops.
   • It should also include a range of doses for a variety of work regimes.
   • The sell-by date and ensure that the supplement has been stored correctly. It must not be in direct sunlight or by heaters or in damp conditions otherwise it will lose nutritional value very quickly.
   • The pack can be resealed easily and is waterproof.
   • Read the instructions and follow them carefully!

This may seem a laborious task but it is worth the effort as this information reduces the risk of you overdosing on certain nutrients, and it should make your selection less confusing and result in you choosing the best supplement for your horse.

COMMON FEED SUPPLEMENTS ON THE MARKET

Salt
This is the most common and the cheapest supplement! Working horses need about 40 g per day added to the feed especially in the summer or humid weather. The easiest way to provide salt in the diet is to use a lick in the stable or field. If horses are seen to be eating soil, licking woodwork or chewing wood it is likely that they are deficient in salt.

Calcium
If feeding cereals such as barley, oats and hay it is essential to add a calcium supplement. If using limestone flour then 25–30 g is a minimum daily requirement. If the horse is young or pregnant you will need a higher calcium level in the supplement than if the horse is fully grown.

Vitamins and minerals
You can purchase either a spectrum supplement that covers the main vitamins and minerals, which can be useful if the horse is stabled and on a grain and hay diet, or you can buy individual vitamins or minerals if you only need to supplement on a specific mineral or vitamin.

If the horse is fully stabled he is likely to need vitamins A, D and E especially in the winter months. A horse being fed a high fat diet will need a vitamin E supplement. If the horse is competing and under stress he could need extra B vitamins especially if the diet has a high ratio of concentrates. A horse that does not get any grass or is on poor grazing is likely to be deficient in the trace elements copper, selenium, manganese, iodine and zinc.

Probiotics

These supplements contain live bacteria and are fed to replace or assist the horse's natural gut microbes when digesting feed. They can increase the horse's effectiveness of fibre fermentation and can be useful in cases of diarrhoea, scouring of foals and for replacing the gut bacteria lost when a horse has been on a course of antibiotics.

Electrolytes

These are substances that are present in the body's fluids. They are responsible for conducting electrical impulses through the body, for example, the muscles contracting and nerve impulses. The major electrolytes are sodium, chloride, potassium, calcium and magnesium. A well fed horse will normally receive the required amount of these electrolytes from the feed but certain conditions such as stress, heavy sweating and diarrhoea increase the demand and this is when supplementation may be necessary. A horse can lose up to 12 litres (2 gallons) of sweat an hour, and these lost electrolytes need to be replaced. Electrolytes can assist in the prevention of dehydration and are offered to endurance horses during rides as they encourage a horse to keep drinking. They can be provided to the horse in the water or feed, or both.

Enzymes

It is claimed that enzymes improve the digestibility of the feed so that the horse can gain more from the feed provided. They can help improve condition and reduce digestive disturbances.

Amino acids

If a growing horse or performance horse is not getting a range of high quality proteins in the diet he could need the essential amino acids methionine and lysine. Performance horses that are undergoing strenuous exercise are sometimes fed amino acids as they can improve the muscle repair, lower the heart rate and assist in the generation of energy from fatty acids.

SOME RULES TO FOLLOW WHEN FEEDING A SUPPLEMENT

- Always follow the manufacturer's recommendations. Do not overfeed, giving double doses will not make the supplement work twice as quickly!
- Split the supplement over all the feeds given to the horse each day as it ensures that the diet remains the same.
- Introduce all supplements gradually. Begin by adding a very small amount to the diet and build up to the required dose over two weeks.
- If you are using the supplement in a hot feed allow it to cool before adding it as some nutrients can be destroyed by heat.
- Ensure the supplement is stored correctly. Incorrect storage can lead to the destruction of the nutrients you are hoping to feed.

HOW SUPPLEMENTS CAN BE FED

Supplements come in a variety of forms and you need to decide which form is best for your horse. Common forms are:

Powder:
Mixed into feed. Some fussy eaters may not eat it in the feed. It should be put into *every* feed not just one per day.

Liquid:
Easier to mix into feeds and usually sweet so the horse tends to eat it. Dispensed using a pump which can be easier than using scoops.

Pellets
Or meal: the nutrients have been added to bran or wheatfeed making it easier to mix into the feeds.

Injections:
Some supplements are given by injection. It tends to be only vitamins such as B12 that are given this way and is a short term 'fix'.

HERBS: THE NATURAL SUPPLEMENT

Herbal supplements are making a strong comeback in the diet of horses and can be a very beneficial natural alternative to the commercial supplements available. Many years ago knowledgeable horsemen (and women) made use of a wide variety of herbs and wild flowers in the diets of their horses and when treating health problems but for some reason this trend died out and has only recently come back into fashion.

Herbs are now being grown by horse owners so that they can
be fed fresh to the horse

The great advantage herbs and flowers have over chemical supplements is that they are completely natural. They will not infringe any drug rules or regulations and tend not to have any detrimental side effects that can be associated with chemicals. If a horse were able to roam over vast acres of untouched pasture land he would probably help himself to many of the herbs and flowers that are used in supplements but as this is not always possible we have to provide them in the diet.

Feeding herbs

Herbs are plants that grow very deep roots and absorb a wide variety of nutrients from the soil. Each herb contains certain substances that are said to be beneficial for the health of the horse and many of these naturally occurring substances are also used in conventional medicines. The substances found in the herbs are released slowly into the system of the horse and in very small quantities. The effects are cumulative so when fed regularly the strength of the substance gradually builds allowing the horse to become accustomed to the supplement without causing imbalances. The principle behind any herbal treatments is little and often. Feeding large amounts has no effect on the speed or effectiveness of the supplement and can lead to overdosing.

Herbal treatments

There are numerous ways to feed herbs to your horse and there are many specialists who have a vast knowledge of the action and effect of all the herbs and can prescribe the correct type for a specific problem. When a horse is ill or under stress the body becomes unbalanced and deficiencies occur. Herbs are used to redress these imbalances and have an effect on the whole body so it is essential to prescribe the correct ones if you are to have any success.

Some examples of common remedial conditions treated by herbs are:

Pain relief	Analgesic herbs
Swellings	Anti-inflammatory herbs
Coughing and soothe contractions	Antispasmodic herbs
Encourage healing	Cell proliferate herbs
Calming	Nervine herbs
Digestive problems	Bitter herbs
Stimulate mucous membranes	Aromatic herbs
Reduce fevers	Febrifuge herbs
Stop bleeding	Hemostatic herbs
Stimulate the body	Tonic herbs
Expelling worms	Vermufuge herbs

When being used as a feed supplement, herbs are chosen for their nutritional content rather than their remedial effects and again each herb needs to be carefully selected on nutritional content in order to fulfil effectively the horse's particular requirement. The great advantages of feeding fresh herbs over chemical supplements are:

- If you grow your own they are readily available.
- They are fresh and natural.
- They are cheaper to buy.
- If grown in the pasture the horse can select his own.

There is a problem in that you do need to learn about the herbs and keep them alive, so if you are not very green-fingered you may prefer to buy in herbal or chemical supplements instead!

Some horse owners grow a selection of common herbs and cut then daily to make up a 'salad' of herbs which is offered to the horse. This allows the horse to choose what they would like to eat. When using this 'pick your own' system you often find the horse choosing to eat different herbs at different times.

Herbs can be offered to the horse in a variety of forms:

- In the pasture.
- Grown, cut and fed fresh each day.
- Cut and put into an infusion (boiled in water).
- Fed dried. When herbs are dried or allowed to wilt they lose some of their nutritional value but drying does mean they can be stored
- Fed as homeopathic pills.
- Fed as bach flower remedies.
- Used in a poultice or compress.

A variety of feed manufacturers such as Hilton Herbs, and Dodson and Horrell are manufacturing dried herbal supplements for specific problems.

Common herbs used as supplements

Comfrey: Symphytum Officinale
A perennial plant that has dark hairy leaves and thick roots. Flowers in early summer. Found in wet soils but will grow in most places if well watered.

Comfrey

This herb contains a mucilage which acts like mucus to protect the stomach lining. It is a highly nutritious herb rich in many vitamins and minerals especially calcium, potassium, iron and the B vitamins. It has healing qualities so can be applied externally to strains and wounds. It is said to help mend fractured bones and can assist horses suffering from arthritis and rheumatism. Recent studies have indicated that overfeeding comfrey can be toxic, so care must be taken when feeding.

Garlic: Allium sativum

Garlic is a member of the onion family and the roots contain the cloves used in the feed. It is an anti-bacterial herb that is rich in sulphur, B vitamins and trace minerals. It is a valuable broad spectrum herb for maintaining health and condition but is especially useful when a horse is suffering from respiratory disorders, blood problems, laminitis, sweet itch and as a fly repellent in the summer.

Fenugreek: Trigonella foenumgraecum

This is an annual plant that has whitish flowers in the summer. It produces seed pods and the seeds are fed to the horse. It is rich in oils, protein and vitamin E. It is an excellent conditioner and is useful for horses that need to put on weight. It is also an effective tonic herb for improving general condition and can promote a good milk yield in lactating mares.

Red clover: Trifolium pratense

Red clover is commonly seen in pasture land. It has distinctive three-leaf clusters (or four leaves if you are very lucky!) and purple or white flowers. It is very nutritious and rich in protein, calcium and other vitamins and minerals. Red clover is an excellent fattening herb and is said to promote a healthy coat and skin. It is said to have a calming effect and is fed to competition horses who 'hot up' at an event.

Dandelion: Taraxacum officinale

This is often considered as a weed and grows everywhere. It has a long tap root and grows yellow flowers throughout the spring and summer. Dandelion is an excellent source of potassium and vitamins B and C. It has diuretic (encourages urination) properties which make it an effective cleanser. It can be fed as a tonic to promote health as it stimulates the kidneys and gall bladder. It can be useful treatment for liver and urinary complaints.

Peppermint: Mentha piperata

This herb is often associated with horses and because of its taste is a very useful addition to the feed of a fussy eater. It has small green leaves and white flowers and can be recognised by the smell of the leaves. Mint is excellent for improving digestion and can aid digestive disturbances and the build-up of gases. It is commonly used as an inhalant when a horse is suffering from a cold as the menthol oil helps clear the airways. It can be useful in the case of ringworm as it has anti-fungal qualities and is a very effective general appetiser.

Using herbs

Herbs can be purchased dried from many health food shops and some equine mixes are made by feed manufacturers. If you wish to grow your own you can buy herb seedlings at most garden centres. Some grass seed mixes now contain herbs, which can be a useful way to add fresh herbs into your grazing land.

Making a herbal infusion

To make an infusion of herbs you need either 15 g of dried herbs or 30 g of fresh herbs. Place the herbs in a jug and pour a pint of boiling water over them. Cover the jug and leave to stand for 5–10 minutes. Strain out the liquid and add it to the horse's feed.

Making a compress/poultice

Bring one or two heaped tablespoons of a herb to the boil in a cup of water. Allow to stand for five minutes then pour the mixture onto a large piece of cottonwool or gauze. When cool enough, apply to the affected part and cover with a bandage. Replace when the compress has become cold. If you wish to make a herbal poultice simply mix the herbal liquid into a paste with bran or flour and spread onto gauze before applying to the affected part.

HOMEOPATHY

Homeopathy is another way of providing herbs to a horse but is used to remedy diseases and problems rather than as a feed supplement. Homeopathy works on the principle that 'like cures like' so a substance which is known to cause certain symptoms in a healthy body is given in diluted form to an individual who is unhealthy and showing the same symptoms. A very small amount of a particular plant is diluted and put into pills, creams or lotions for internal or external application, depending on the particular problem.

Like herbalism, homeopathic remedies act gradually on the whole body so they do not cause any side effects. Many horse owners are now turning to homeopathy as an alternative to conventional medicines as they can be used on competition horses since they are not banned, are natural and the horse suffers no side effects.

It is essential when using homeopathy to understand what you are giving your horse as some remedies can have a powerful effect and it may not be what you expected! If you are in need of anything more than the basic first aid remedies listed overleaf you should consult a homeopathic specialist. A good homeopath and ideally a homeopathic vet will know exactly what remedies are required for your horse's particular problem and can prescribe the correct dosages.

Common homeopathic remedies

These are available in most chemists and healthfood shops. Choose the best remedy for the particular problem, but do not be tempted to give several remedies in case one is better than another.

Arnica

In tablet, lotion or creams. Only use externally if skin is not broken.

This remedy is very useful to give a horse immediately after some kind of injury, surgery or trauma. It is ideal for bruising, swelling, stiffness and strains or sprains. It should be used at 30 potency for the first week then 6 potency until symptoms clear.

Aconite

In tablet or liquid form. This is used to relieve pain and nervous tension. It can also help in the treatment of shock immediately after injury. If given early enough it can help reduce fevers.

Calendula

In tablets or creams and lotions. This is an excellent treatment for any open wounds as it encourages healing.

Hypericum

In tablet form or cream and lotions. This remedy is a very useful treatment for grazes and broken skin, especially if nerve endings are bruised or damaged. It has some pain relieving qualities and helps to flush out puncture wounds.

Rhus tox

This remedy is very effective when a horse is suffering from stiffness in joints which is worse in cold, damp weather. It reduces inflammation in tendons and liga-ments and is useful for horses suffering from rheumatism and arthritis.

BACH FLOWER REMEDIES

Bach flower remedies work on the same principles of homeopathy in that they contain small quantities of herbs that re-balance the body and therefore remedy disease. They come in liquid form and are fed to the horse by putting four drops onto a slice of apple or ten drops into the water bucket each day until the symp-toms disappear.

There are thirty-eight remedies that are prescribed depending on the characteristics that the patient is demonstrating. As the majority of books written are based on human characteristics this can often lead to a misdiagnosis when translating them into horse characteristics. This is where a specialist can be very useful in deciding which of these remedies suit your horse's specific problems.

The most common bach flower remedy used is the rescue remedy (in liquid or cream) which can be given to the horse or rider when they are suffering from stress, injury or trauma. It is a blend of five flower remedies which relieve the symptoms of shock, fear, panic, stress and tension, and has been found to be very effective. A useful addition to any first aid kit for both the horse and rider!

Century and Mimulus have also been very effective in calming down nervous or fretful horses.

SELECTING THE CORRECT FEED SUPPLEMENT

If you feel that your horse's diet is deficient in particular nutrients and want to feed a supplement the following information can assist you when deciding what supplement to choose.

1. Note down the mineral and vitamin content of the horse's daily feed: concentrate and hay (if a figure is not available then use the nutritional charts in Chapter 3).
2. Note down your horse's specific mineral and vitamin requirements from the charts below and tick which ones are met by the feed.
3. Decide which minerals and vitamins are lacking.
4. From the supplements available choose the best one that replaces these missing vitamins or minerals.

Recommended daily amounts

Table 10.1 Vitamins: A, D, E and K

Name horse	Maintenance	Light work	Medium work	Hard work	Pregnant and lactating mare	Growing
A: Retinol	30 iu/kg of bodyweight	30 iu/kg of bodyweight	45 iu/kg of bodyweight	45 iu/kg of bodyweight	60 iu/kg of bodyweight	45 iu/kg of bodyweight
D: Calciferol	1,200 iu/kg of feed (dry matter)	1,250–1,300 iu/kg of feed (dry matter)	1,300–1,500 iu/kg of feed (dry matter)	1,500–2,000 iu/kg of feed (dry matter)	2,000 iu/kg of feed (dry matter)	2,000 iu/kg of feed (dry matter)
E: Tocopherol	50–80 iu/kg of dry matter	50–80 iu/kg of dry matter	50–80 iu/kg of dry matter	80–100 iu/kg of dry matter	100 iu/kg of dry matter	100 iu/kg of dry matter
K	No exact figures are known					

Table 10.2 Vitamins: B complex

Name	Requirements	Sources
B1: Thiamin	Exact requirements are not known. 3–5 mg/kg dry matter should be sufficient.	Green forage. Good hay. Made by microflora in intestines. Cereal grains. Brewer's yeast. Herb sources: alfalfa, dandelion, garlic, fenugreek, red clover, hawthorn.
B2: Riboflavin	No more than 2 milligrams per kg of dry matter per day.	Green forage. Good hay. Made by microflora in intestines. Milk and milk products. Herb sources: alfalfa, dandelion, garlic, fenugreek, red clover, hawthorn.
B3: Niacin	No specific requirements have been determined. Up to 400 mg a day.	Green forage especially lucerne. Oil seeds. Made by microflora in intestines. Herb sources: alfalfa, dandelion, garlic, fenugreek, red clover, hawthorn.
B5: Pantothenic acid	No specific requirements have been determined.	Green forage. Cereals and peas. Made by microflora in intestines. Up to 100 mg a day. Herb sources: alfalfa, dandelion, garlic, fenugreek, red clover, hawthorn, kelp.
B6: Pyridoxine	No specific requirements have been determined. 25–50 mg a day. Heavily worked horses have benefited from B6 supplementation.	Green forage. Cereal grains. Made by the microflora in the caecum and colon. Herb sources: alfalfa, dandelion, garlic, fenugreek, red clover, hawthorn, kelp.
B12: Cyanocobalamin	No specific requirements have been determined. Usually 4–10 micrograms per pound are fed when supplementation is required.	Made by the microflora in the caecum and colon. Green forages.
Biotin	10–30 milligrams daily for 6–9 months to improve hoof condition.	Made by the microflora in caecum. Yeast. Green forage. Cereals.
Choline	If supplementation is required a dose of 500 milligrams is sufficient for a 500–600 kg horse.	Natural fats. Green leafy forage. Yeast. Cereals. Sugarbeet. Whole oats. Alfalfa.
Folic acid	20 milligrams daily may be beneficial to stabled competition horses in hard work.	Green, leafy forage. Made by the microflora in caecum.

NUTRITION AND THE FEEDING OF HORSES

Table 10.3 Daily mineral requirements of the horse

Name	Maintenance for 500 kg horse	Working horses	Pregnant and lactating mares	Yearlings	2 year olds
Calcium	25 g limestone 65 g	25–40 g limestone 65–105 g	33 g limestone 93 g	32 g limestone 88 g	28 g limestone 78 g
Phosphorous	19 g	18–29 g	26–28 g pregnant 22–36 g lactating	15–20 g	13 g
Magnesium	7–8 g	9–15 g	9 g pregnant 9–11g lactating	5.5–9.0 g	7 g
Sulphur	0.15% of total diet	0.15% of total diet	0.15% of total diet	0.15% of total diet	0.15% of total diet
Sodium chloride	0.1% of total diet (44 g)	0.1% of total diet	0.1% of total diet	0.1% of total diet	0.1% of total diet
Potassium	25 g	31–50 g	29–31 g pregnant 33–46 g lactating	18 g	23 g
Cobalt	0.1 mg/kg	0.1 mg/kg	0.1 mg/kg	0.1 mg/kg	0.1 mg/kg
Zinc	40 mg/kg	40 mg/kg	40 mg/kg	40 mg/kg	40 mg/kg
Copper	10 mg/kg	10 mg/kg	10 mg/kg	10 mg/kg	10 mg/kg
Manganese	40 mg/kg	40 mg/kg	40 mg/kg	40 mg/kg	40 mg/kg

mg/kg = milligrams per kilogram of total diet

CHAPTER 11

Feed Tips, Problems and Possible Solutions

This chapter covers the more common feed problems and some possible solutions that have been successful. Of course you should always remember that every horse is an individual and each problem must be dealt with accordingly.

COMMON PROBLEMS

Sharp teeth

Horses being given concentrate feeds and hay can develop sharp edges on the molars which can lead to mouth problems such as lacerated cheeks and tongue. An easy way to check for sharp teeth is to gently press the sides of the mouth along the teeth edges. If the horse pulls away and shows discomfort it is likely that there are sharp edges on the teeth which are causing discomfort. The presence of whole grains or lengths of hay longer than 25–30 cm in the droppings can be a sign of sharp teeth or the horse bolting his feed.

Possible reasons for a horse losing condition

- Sharp teeth can lead to a loss of condition as the horse feels discomfort when chewing.
- Worm burden can lead to a loss of condition and weight so ensure your horse is being wormed regularly and if you are concerned consult your vet.
- Feeding a poor diet. This could be due to poor quality feeds, low energy feeds or not enough feed so ensure your horse's diet is balanced and fulfils your horse's individual requirements.
- Temperament: A highly-strung horse can expend twice as much energy during exercise as their calmer counterparts and this must be taken into consideration when designing their ration.

Feeding a fussy eater

Many nervy horses tend to do better if fed in the evening when things have quietened down. Offer a fussy horse small frequent meals (4 or 5) rather than two or three larger meals. Ensure your horse is comfortable and content: low-grade muscle soreness or discomfort can put horses off their feed. Placing a few drops of peppermint or vanilla essence in the feed can encourage a fussy horse to eat and

197

avoid any problems with sugar content from molasses. Always feed at the same times every day and use the same bucket which is thoroughly cleaned out after each feed.

It is essential to also try and address the reason for the horse being fretful and off his food.

Fats and vitamin E

If boosting the energy content of a feed with oils always check the vitamin E content in the feed, the amounts below act as a guide:

4 oz of oil	1,000 iu vitamin E
8 oz of oil	1,200 iu vitamin E
12 oz of oil	1,400 iu vitamin E
16 oz of oil	1,600 iu vitamin E

Impatience while feeding

Some horses get very wound up when waiting for their feed. They may paw, kick the door, strike the walls or weave, all in anticipation of their feed. This can lead to the horse being stressed just prior to eating, which will not help digestion and can also be damaging to the horse and the stable. The most straightforward solution is to feed these horses first as once they are eating the problem is solved! Always check the horse is being fed enough roughage as the impatience may be due to hunger.

Bolting feed

This refers to those horses who dive into the feed bucket and have cleaned up within minutes. They do very little chewing, which can lead to colic, choke and diarrhoea. This bolting of the feed can be caused by:

- Irregular feed times so that the horse is very hungry when fed.
- Feeding a group of horses together. The more aggressive ones take over the meals of the passive horses after they have eaten theirs.
- Tooth problems which cause the horse discomfort when chewing.

If you know it is not a tooth problem then placing chaff in the feed can increase chewing time and so slow down the speed of eating. Placing a large, smooth stone on the feed bucket so that the horse has to eat around it can slow the speed of eating and feeding the hay first takes the edge off a horse's appetite if it is very hungry.

Aggression when feeding

Some horses are known to show aggressive tendencies during feeding. The aggressiveness may be directed at the handler or other horses. Handlers can avoid dealing with the horse while he is eating but it can be problematic for the horses in the stables next door. In the worst case they can go off their feed in fear of being harassed by the more aggressive horse. This is common in indoor yards with bars between the stables. The aggressive behaviour is more problematic if feeding horses in the field. The aggressive horse will often chase the more passive horses away from the feed and it can lead to kicking and fighting during feedtimes.

A horse that is aggressive when eating should be taken out of the field and given his feed separately. If the horse is stabled then ensure he is not affecting the horses in the adjacent stables, if he is then a rearrangement of the stabling may be required. To avoid aggressive behaviour the following points should be considered:

- Allow the horse to eat in peace.
- Do not take the feed away until the horse has finished.
- Avoid competitive feed situations.
- Always ensure enough feed is available if feeding a group of horses.

Eating manure

Manure eating is a habit some stabled horses develop. It can also be seen in foals and is thought to be a way of a foal developing gut bacteria to assist the digestion of roughages. In the mature horse it is much more likely to be due to boredom or a deficiency in minerals or fibre. Irregular feed times, lack of fibre and hunger can increase the problem. It can be difficult to break the habit as the horse needs to be occupied when stabled. Provide good quality hay between feeds, especially overnight to keep the horse occupied. Check the mineral requirement and ensure you are fulfilling this need in the diet. Turning the horse out to grass can break the habit and if all else fails the horse may need to be muzzled between meals.

Chewing wood

This is another habit often associated with the bored stabled horse. Like manure eating, irregular feed times and low roughage diets increase the problem. Some people feel that wood chewing can be a symptom of a phosphorous deficiency and feeding sweet feeds also tends to increase the habit. A lack of fibre is a common cause. Studies carried out on wood chewing revealed that field-kept horses tend to chew wood more frequently in the spring and by feeding hay to these horses the incidents of chewing was reduced.

There are a number of possible remedies for wood chewing:
- Increase the fibre content of the feed.
- Reduce boredom in stabled horses.
- Feed at regular times.
- Provide a balanced ration.
- Coat the wood with a bitter tasting preparation as a deterrent.
- Protect the wood in stables with metal strips.

Windsucking

This term describes the habit developed by a horse of grabbing onto something with the front teeth, arching its neck and gulping in air. Some horse are so practised at it that they can windsuck without holding anything in their teeth. Once a horse has developed this vice it is virtually impossible to break it. Windsucking causes dietary problems, excessive wear of the incisor teeth and poor condition. Windsucking horses are often difficult to keep weight on as they have little appetite. The air sucked in by the horse give it a false 'full' feeling which stops them eating their feed. The most successful methods for preventing a horse from windsucking are:

- To turn the horse out at grass to minimise the boredom.
- For the horse to wear a windsucking collar that fits snugly around the throat.

Mane and tail chewing

This habit is most common in young horses particularly weanlings and youngsters confined to a barn or small paddock. It is thought to be due to a lack of minerals especially salt, phosphorous and copper, or a lack of fibre in the diet. Chewing hair can lead to digestive disturbances, obstructions and lacerated gums. To prevent this habit occurring ensure plenty of roughage is fed at regular intervals and a horse that has developed this habit can be deterred by smearing the tails or manes of the other horses with a bitter tasting preparation.

COMMON QUESTIONS ANSWERED

How can the nutrient value of feeds be assessed?

The most effective way to find out the nutritional value of your feeds is to have them analysed. Most feed companies will carry out a feed analysis which will provide details of the nutrient levels present in the sample. This test can be carried out on roughages and concentrate feeds.

Which plants in the pasture could be poisonous to horses?

Table 11.1 Common poisonous plants found in pasture land

Plant	Toxic compound	Amount	Symptoms
Ragwort	Alkaloids	Cumulative effect	Weight loss, colic, drowsiness, liver damage, jaundice.
Horsetail	Thiaminase	Cumulative	Weight loss, incoordination, staggering, trembling, collapse.

Plant	Toxic compound	Amount	Symptoms
Bracken fern	Thiaminase	Cumulative over 30–60 days	Weight loss, inco-ordination, staggering, trembling, collapse.
St John's Wort	Photosensitising agent	Large amounts	Sunburn type lesions on the skin
Deadly nightshade	Alkaloid Salanine	1–10 lb	Depression, diarrhoea and colic.
Poison Hemlock	Cardiac glycosides	Small amount	Colic, diarrhoea, shock, death within 24 hours.
Foxglove	Cardiac glycosides	Small amount	Colic, diarrhoea, shock, death within 24 hours.

How should you feed a horse that is travelling?

Horses that are travelling over long distances or for more than six hours should be provided with concentrate feed as well as good quality hay. Travelling can cause stress in horses leading to diarrhoea and in some cases laminitis. Over recent years there has also been an increase of travel sickness, and lung disease (pleuropneumonia) has developed in horses travelling long distances.

As the horse is standing still during the journey high energy concentrates need to be avoided as they are likely to lead to metabolic problems such as filled legs. The best feed solution is to offer plenty of good quality hay (damped down) and small amounts of an easily digested concentrate feed such as a low energy mix (damped down) or a barley mash.

To avoid travel stress and related health problems these points should be followed:

- Damp down all feed offered to the horse.
- Ensure there is adequate ventilation but no draughts.
- If it is safe to do so, unload every 3–4 hours for 20 minutes to walk around and rest.
- Do not tie the horse too short. If the head is tied up above the backline it prevents the drainage of mucus from the respiratory tract.
- Check the horse regularly for signs of dehydration and give electrolytes in the feed.
- Offer the horse fresh water regularly, especially if the weather is hot and dry.

How can you reduce the dust in the feed?

- Dampen down the feed with water or sugarbeet.
- If using grains make sure they are fresh as dust increases in grains that are stored for more than a few days.
- Only use good quality feeds as they will contain less dust.
- Ensure feeds are stored correctly as deterioration leads to a build-up of dusts and spores.

How can I improve the condition and colour of my horse's coat?

- Feed 5 ml (1–2 teaspoons) of corn oil per 45 kg of bodyweight.
- Ensure your horse is receiving adequate amounts of vitamin A, iron, copper and zinc in the feed.
- An increase in protein has an influence on the depth of colour in the coat. To improve a poor coat linseed can be fed twice a week.

Can weak, chalky hooves be improved through feeding?

This depends on the reason for the hooves being in poor condition. In some cases a dietary deficiency can result in cracked, weak hooves. This may be remedied by feeding a supplement that contains high quality protein, calcium and 15 mg of biotin each day.

Appendix

Table A1 Daily nutrient requirements of working horses

Weight (kg)	Type of work	MJDE	Crude protein (g)	Lysine (g)	Calcium (g)	Phosphorous (g)	Potassium (g)
200	Rest	30	296	10	8	6	10
	Light	39	370	13	11	8	14
	Medium	47	444	16	14	10	17
	Hard	63	592	21	18	13	22
300	Rest	44	416	16	12	8.5	15
	Light	55	520	18	16	11.5	19
	Medium	68	640	19	20	14	24
	Hard	89	840	25	26	18.5	29
400	Rest	55	536	19	16	11	20
	Light	71	670	23	20	15	25
	Medium	85	804	28	25	17	31
	Hard	114	1072	38	33	23	40
500	Rest	68	656	23	20	14	25
	Light	87	820	29	25	18	31
	Medium	104	884	34	30	21	37
	Hard	139	1312	46	40	29	50
600	Rest	80	776	27	24	17	35
	Light	103	970	34	30	21	36
	Medium	123	1164	41	36	25	44
	Hard	164	1552	54	47	34	59
700	Rest	88	851	30	28	20	35
	Light	113	1064	37	32	23	40
	Medium	135	1277	45	39	28	48
	Hard	181	1702	60	52	37	65

Adapted from Nutritional Requirements of Horses.

Table A2 Daily nutrient requirements of pregnant mares

Weight (kg)	Month	MJDE	Crude protein (g)	Lysine (g)	Calcium (g)	Phosphorous (g)	Potassium (g)
200	9	35	361	13	16	12	13
	10	36	368	13	16	12	13
	11	38	391	14	17	13	14
400	9	63	654	23	28	21	24
	10	64	666	23	29	22	24
	11	68	708	25	31	23	26
500	9	77	801	28	35	26	29
	10	78	815	29	35	27	30
	11	83	866	30	37	28	31
600	9	91	947	33	41	31	34
	10	93	965	34	42	32	35
	11	99	1024	36	44	34	37
700	9	100	1039	36	45	34	38
	10	102	1058	37	46	35	39
	11	108	1124	39	49	37	50

Adapted from Nutritional Requirements of Horses

Table A3 Daily nutrient requirements of lactating mares

Weight (kg)	Month	MJDE	Crude protein (g)	Lysine (g)	Calcium (g)	Phosphorous (g)	Potassium (g)
200	First 3 months	58	688	24	27	18	21
	Until weaning	52	528	18	18	11	15
400	First 3 months	97	1141	40	45	29	37
	Until weaning	83	839	29	29	18	26
500	First 3 months	120	1427	50	56	36	46
	Until weaning	103	1048	37	36	22	33
600	First 3 months	143	1711	60	67	43	55
	Until weaning	122	1258	44	43	27	40
700	First 3 months	161	1997	70	78	51	64
	Until weaning	137	1468	51	50	31	46

Adapted from Nutritional Requirements of Horses

Table A4 Daily nutrient requirements of the yearling

Est Weight (kg)	Month	MJDE	Crude protein (g)	Lysine (g)	Calcium (g)	Phosphorous (g)	Potassium (g)
200	12	Average growth	37	392	17	12	7
		Rapid growth	44	462	19	15	8
	18	Average growth	35	357	16	10	6
400	12	Average growth	66	700	30	23	13
		Rapid growth	72	770	33	27	15
	18	Average growth	67	716	30	21	12
500	12	Average growth	80	851	36	29	16
		Rapid growth	90	956	40	34	19
	18	Average growth	84	893	38	27	15
600	12	Average growth	96	1023	43	36	20
		Rapid growth	106	1127	48	41	22
	18	Average growth	101	1077	45	33	18
700	12	Average growth	111	1176	50	39	22
		Rapid growth	121	1281	54	44	24
	18	Average growth	114	1215	51	37	20

Adapted from Nutritional Requirements of Horses

Bibliography

Bromiley, M. (1994) *Natural Methods for Equine Health* (Oxford: Blackwell Scientific Publications)

Clarke, A. (1988) *Mycology of Silage and Mycotoxicosis in Silage and Health* (Marlow: Chalcombe Publications)

Equine Research Inc (1992) *Feeding to Win* (Texas, USA: Equine Research Inc)

Frape, D. (1990) *Equine Nutrition and Feeding* (Harlow: Longman Scientific & Technical)

Holland, T. (1995) 'Hay (there's no need to panic)', *Your Horse Magazine*, September

Holland, T. (1995) 'Choosing a Feed', *Your Horse Magazine*, November

Johnson, T. (1993) 'Old-fashioned methods merge with modern ideas', *Horse and Hound*, 2 September

Kohnke, J. (1992) *Feeding and Nutrition* (New South Water, Australia: Birubi Pacific)

Lewis, L. (1996) *Feeding and Care of the Horse*, second edition (Philadelphia, USA: Williams & Wilkins)
Marlin, D. (1996) 'Salts for survival,' *Your Horse Magazine*, August

Pilliner, S. (1993) *Horse Nutrition and Feeding* (Oxford: Blackwell Scientific Publications)

Smith, T. (1894) *Homeopathic Medicine* (Northampton: Thorsons Publishers Limited)

Vogel, C. (1991) 'New approach removes guesswork', *Horse and Hound*, 22 August

National Research Council (1989) *Nutritional Requirements of Horses*, Fifth Edition Revised (Washington DC: National Academy Press)

Rossdale, P. (1976) *Inside the Horse* (Salt Lake City: Desert News Press)

Useful addresses

The British Horse Society
The British Equestrian Centre
Stoneleigh
Kenilworth
Warwickshire
CV8 2LR

The Faculty of Homeopathy
2 Powis Place
Great Ormond Street
London
WC1N 3HJ

Feed companies

Allen and Page Norfolk Horsefeeds
Norfolk Mill
Shipdham Airfield
Thetford
Norfolk
IP25 7SD

Baileys Horse Feeds
Four Elms Mills
Bardfield Saling
Braintree
Essex
CM7 5EJ

Clark and Butcher Ltd
Lion Mills
Soham
Ely
Cambridge
CB7 5HY

Dengie Crop Driers Ltd
Hall Road
Asheldham
Southminster
Essex
CM0 7JF

Dodson & Horrell Ltd
Ringstead
Kettering
Northants
NN14 4BX

Equibury Feeds
Edgewarebury Lane
Edgeware
Middlesex
HA8 8QS

Hilton Herbs
Downclose Farm
Downclose Lane
North Perrott
Crewkerne
Somerset
TA18 7SH

Marksway Horsehage
Marldon
Paignton
Devon
TQ3 1SP

Natural Animal Feeds Ltd
Penrhos
Raglan
Gwent
NP5 2DJ

Saracen Horse Feeds
Pledge Animal Feeds
Stewarts Farm
Stanford Rivers
Ongar
Essex

Spillers Horse Feeds
Old Wolverton Road
Old Wolverton
Milton Keynes
MK12 5PZ

Triple Crown Feeds
12 Dukes Court
Bognor Road
Chichester
West Sussex
PO19 2FX

Index

peppermint, 197
perennial ryegrass, 83
performance energy, 127
peyer's patches, 114
pharynx, 110
phenylalanine, 32
phosphorous, 29, 38, 45
photosynthesis, 25
phylloquinone, 41
plants, 20, 25, 28
poisoning, 38, 200
polysaccharides, 28
potassium, 45, 53
pregnancy, 145
pregnant mare, 130
probiotics, 182
protein, 9, 14, 15, 24, 29, 118, 128, 142
prothrombin, 39

quiet mix, 73

racehorse cubes, 78
ragwort, 86, 200
rats, 103
rectum, 117
red clover, 190
repair of tissues, 29
retinol, 37
rhus tox, 192
riboflavin, 42
roughage feeds, 82

salivary glands, 109
salt, 184
sand colic, 52
scouring, 185
seed hay, 83, 141
selenium, 39
show pony, 176
showjumper, 148, 175
silage, 88, 141
simple carbohydrates, 27
    sugars, 27
small colon, 117
    intestine, 113

sodium, 53
    chloride, 45
soft palate, 110
soyabean, 65
    meal, 33
spore, 87, 201
stallion, 133
starch, 28
steam flaking, 97
stomach, 111
straw, 91
streams, 51
stress, 198
stud mix, 80
    stock, 39
sublingual gland, 109
submaxillary gland, 109
sugarbeet, 62, 72, 143
sulphur, 29, 45
sunlight, 102
supplement, 181

tail chewing, 200
taste buds, 110
teeth, 107, 108, 197
temperament, 17
tendons, 30
thiamine, 42
thoroughbred, 172
threonine, 32
thumps, 147
Timothy grass, 33, 83
tocopherol, 40
tongue, 110
toxicity, 37
trachea, 110
travelling, 201
trickle feeders, 11
trypsin, 114
tryptophan, 32

unsaturated fats, 35

valine, 32
vegetable oil, 36, 66